SEXUALITY AND SPIRITUALITY, PURSUING INTEGRATION

William F. Kraft, Ph.D.

Wipf & Stock Publishers
Eugene, Oregon

Wipf & Stock Publishers
199 West 8th Avenue, Suite 3
Eugene, OR 97401

Sexuality and Spirituality,
Pursuing Integration
Copyright©2005 William F. Kraft, Ph.D.
ISBN: 1-59752-150-7
Publication Date: May 2005

10   9   8   7   6   5   4   3   2   1

For
Kylie and Bill

TABLE OF CONTENTS

PREFACE

Over four decades, many men and women have shared their intimate lives with me. Whether these people were educated in the "old days" before the 1960's or in the more recent "new days," they often experienced sexuality as problematic or disappointing.

Most of these clients, colleagues, and friends were formed and informed according to fragmented rather than wholistic paradigms of sexuality. Many of their approaches maximized the biology and psychology of sexuality, while minimizing or excluding its spiritual dimensions. Although such models were (and are) popular, practical, and easily learned they still lack the depth and values necessary to practice healthy and holy sexuality.

Other models have focused on moral standards for sexual behavior, while lacking empirical, clinical, and cultural support. These religious, theological, and philosophical approaches offer strong visions for good living, and are often weak in giving concrete ways to implement them. In short, increasingly more people are dissatisfied with these and other modern and postmodern approaches promulgated in mass media, education, and culture.

This book is a response to such questions as: What is sexuality? Spirituality? How are they interrelated? What is healthy sex—and, how can we achieve it? Are there different kinds of sexuality? What are female-male similarities and differences? What is the sense and nonsense of marital and nonmarital sex, heterosexuality, homosexuality, masturbation, sexual addictions, and abstinence?

My goal is to construct a model of sexuality and spirituality that engenders more health and satisfaction. My method is phenomenological. Theological truths are not explicitly included—I am a psychologist, not a theologian. Nevertheless, theologians and religious leaders across a broad spectrum have assured me that my vision is not incongruent with theirs and that it can serve as an infrastructure for their studies. My hope is that what follows will help married, single, and vowed celibate people to cope with, grow from, and enjoy their sexuality.

Gratitude is offered to Pat Frauenholz and Elizabeth Thompson for their patient collaboration and diligent typing. I am especially grateful to the clients, students, friends, family, and God who shared their stories and helped me make secular-and-sacred sense of sex.

CHAPTER ONE
STORIES OF SEX

Everyone can tell stories of sex. Our stories may involve reality and fantasy, love and loneliness, feast and famine—all of these experiences and more. Some of our stories evoke joy and pleasure, while others evoke frustration and pain. Whatever our stories, they tell us something about ourselves as well as influence our lives.

Listen to this thirty-five year old woman. "My divorce was the most difficult thing I've ever done. The pain for me and my kids, and I think for my husband too, was excruciating. Although I never believed in divorce, I felt that a marriage where people were killing each other was worse than any divorce. Sure, it's easy to say now that I got married when I was too young, nineteen. But we did it—and, we had three children.

"It's been three years since my divorce, and things are settling down a bit. I've somehow learned to manage to get by with much less than I previously had, and I think I'm a little more fortunate than many women in that I got a decent job. Still, I'm not paid nearly the same as a man doing a comparable job. I resent that, but I've learned that pent-up anger does a lot of harm to everyone, especially me. Nevertheless, we are managing, and I feel we are better off.

"Yes, it's difficult, especially when I get lonely. Sometimes I crave to

1

be intimate. Sometime my desires seem purely physical—almost anybody will do. I want to be close, to touch, to be with someone who loves me. I've had two relationships in the past two years. No, I'm not going down to a bar to be picked up, though I can appreciate women who do. I met a couple of nice guys who proposed that we could have a short-term relationship, and I agreed. We had fun, and it felt good to be touched and to touch. The relationship was not all sexual, but sex was major part of it. When we separated, I felt empty and lonely again.

"Am I destined to go through life having periodic affairs? I hate to call them that; it sounds cheap. They're more than that. But when the relationship is over, I have to admit that I feel empty and depressed. It seems that nothing lasts. Must I be condemned to being lonely and alone?

"I'd like to get married again. But this time, I'm going to be sure; at least I'll try to know what I'm getting into. Still, I'm thirty-five; I'm not old, but I'm not young either. Try to get married when you have three kids and you're over thirty. I really don't know what's going to happen; it scares me. I feel the odds are against me. Sure, I suppose you can get married if you're willing to get married to almost anyone. But I will not travel that road again.

"So what do I do? Do I try to raise my kids, and periodically have some sort of relationship? Do I try to be a single mother? Do I masturbate when needs become intense? Believe me, masturbation is a poor substitute for another person. Can you tell me where I can find an available mature man? Can you tell me what I should do with my yearnings for intimacy? Being alone is lonely. Should I just accept my lot and live through it? Somehow life is too short for that. What should I do? Can you tell me?"

Like many women and men, this woman finds herself in a quandary. Although her relationships give short-term meaning and satisfaction, they fail to promote sustained serenity. Although she desires and enjoys sex, she wants steadfast love even more. She also knows she is growing older, and the odds are against her. She chose to be divorced in lieu of a marital charade, yet she does not want to be single. What chance does she really have? If she remains single, what can she do with her longings for intimacy?

"My parents were not exactly thrilled when I told them I planned to become a nun. They knew I was thinking about entering religious life, but they never thought I would go through with it. Of course, they said they wanted what was best for me, but my plans seemed to disappoint them.

"They asked me if I really knew what I was doing. Was I really willing to give up married life, a husband and children? My parents bluntly asked me if I could be happy and celibate. My first impulse was to confront them with the realities of married life. I could have argued that not many married people are really happy and fulfilled. Neither did I try to convince them that religious life was the best way for me to live and love. Time would tell.

"My older brother shook his head in apparent disgust; my younger sister thought I was stupid. Some of my relatives gave me lukewarm approval, and others just seemed indifferent. My friends pointed out the fun and opportunities I'd be missing. The guy I was dating was really shocked. Although he knew it was coming, he was hurt. And my decision hurt me too; I still get upset when I think about us. But if I didn't at least give religious life like a try, I'd be doing myself and him an injustice. I really couldn't say much, only that I loved him but couldn't marry him.

"All that seems like a thousand years ago; it was twenty-five years ago. A silver jubilee can evoke such memories. Religious life has been good to me; I hope I have been good to it. I have precious friends. I think I've given good service. More importantly, I feel I have grown closer to God and to people. But, my parent's haunting questions come back to me: can I really live a celibate life? The experts say that I am at the peak of my sexual life, and I believe them. I'm at a loss as to what to do with my sexual feelings. Sometimes when I am lonely, I yearn to hold a man and to be held by him. I wonder what it would be like to make love with a man. Although I know that this is contrary to my commitment, I sill have my yearnings to be intimate, my desires to give and to be given to.

"Yes, I know some theories encourage integrating sexuality. But they don't say how. Integration is a nice word; how in God's name do you do it. I tried masturbation, but that really didn't do any good. It did relieve some tension, but it seemed to make things worse. After masturbating, I felt lonelier. I don't have the guilt feelings I had when I was an adolescent, but I sense masturbation is not the best way to cope with my sexuality.

"I am trying to lead a good religious life, and many people say that I do. I am a vowed celibate, but I am also sexual—very much so. Sometimes I feel I am the only one like me, but I know that most sisters have similar feelings to a lesser or greater degree. Still, we seldom if ever talk about it. Sure, we hear lectures and sometimes a few friends will talk, but seldom are the cards put on the table and something concrete done about it. I feel so alone with my sexuality."

Unlike the single parent, this religious sister vowed celibacy. She believes that the religious life is the best way she can live. She is a vibrant woman who loves and serves God and people, but her sexuality is frustrating. She finds herself in situations of collusion where people try to pretend to themselves and to others that sexual issues are unimportant or resolved. Although this sister is given spiritual and psychological formation, she feels that the sexual (incarnational) aspect of her life is given little practical recognition.

"Celibacy, why in the world would somebody choose that? What do people like nuns, brothers, and priests do with their sexuality? My guess is that some masturbate or mess around; others repress it and become irritable and frustrated. Really, I don't know what they do. I don't know how they could be happy or healthy without sex. Isn't celibacy abnormal?

"You could call me a celibate in the sense that I'm not married, but I have an active sex life. Sex is not that difficult to find. There are a lot of lovely, lonely women, and there are a lot of places where they are waiting to have a good time. Besides, increasingly more women are taking the initiative to have sex with no strings attached.

"Yes, I've been married twice. No more of that for me. Much too much hassle, and for what? If I didn't have these damn payments, I'd really be on easy street. Look, I have my own place, sports car, and I go wherever and whenever I want. What's better than having what you want?

"Okay, I know I'm getting older. I'm fifty-two. I guess I have to admit that I'm not what I used to be. But if you have the money and make the effort, you can get most of what you want. Me lonely? I guess I am sometimes, but who isn't? And of course there's always masturbation. Sure, it's not as good as a woman, but it does help, and it's safe. What do I do with my sexuality? What else—I satisfy it."

This man's approach to sex differs radically from the religious sister and the divorced woman. He simply satisfies his sexual desires; he claims to have no problem with sex. Yet, he does admit to loneliness—the presence of a beloved in absence. We will see that this individual and others like him need and even desire the spiritual, that his recreational sex is actually an unconscious but aborted attempt to experience transcendence—healthy union with another.

Consider the thoughts of this sixty-year-old man. "When my wife died, I almost died. It's good to say that we were happy with each other. I was fortunate to have lived with and to have loved such a wonderful woman for thirty-five years, and to have three fine children. I am grateful, but I still feel lost and lonely. Although I know my wife is still with me, I can't really touch and feel, laugh and play with, talk and listen to her. This hurts and hurts and hurts. I feel cheated and get angry when I see people much older than she was. We planned so much and looked forward to enjoying our time together in our later years. Why did she die?

"Although I don't really want to get married again, I find myself reaching out for someone. I think my wife would understand this. When the yearning is intense, I don't know what to do. I know I can enter a relationship that would ease my pain. Alcohol helps, but it only numbs the pain for a while and solves nothing. When I take stock of myself, I wonder if I am strong enough to be celibate, or if I need or want to be.

"What do I do with my longings for intimacy? How do I live with my loneliness? Can I be happy and alone? What do I do when a woman invites me to be intimate with her? It is awfully tempting. Would it be so wrong to enter a relationship? Whom would I be hurting? Some of my colleagues think I'm crazy for not accepting such an invitation. But something in me says no. If I say no, what do I do with my sexual feelings? Better yet, what do I do with my loneliness, with my love? Do I just numb them? I don't like numbing myself; it kills my spirit. What is the answer?"

This man did not choose celibacy; it was thrust upon him. He never planned on leading a single life, nor does he want to. Unlike the religious sister, he did not freely choose to live a celibate life, nor does he live in a community that supports and nourishes him. Unlike the divorced man, he did not choose to be single and does not engage in sexual affairs. More akin to the religious and lay woman than to the single man, this widower also wonders what he should do with his sexuality, with his yearning for intimacy, with his lonely love.

"Well, what do you do with sex if you want to remain celibate? Here I am: twenty-two, almost a college graduate, and still a virgin. I almost feel embarrassed, like I have to apologize because I haven't had sexual relations. Some consider me to be old-fashioned; others don't care; a few value my stand. For various reasons, I think pre-marital sex is wrong for me. It may sound stupid, but I want to wait until marriage. It's a value I want to uphold. Sure, I have to admit I'd like to try it. Sometimes I really get horny, and it's awfully tempting. Why do I feel one way and think another?

"Sure, I'm given the argument that it all depends on the situation. You know—if two people are honest and sincere about their relationship and don't hurt anyone, then what's wrong with having sex. As long as you don't exploit another, sex is okay. They say it's a natural drive that should be satisfied. What am I,—unnatural? I can't give them much of an argument. I can only say that since I wouldn't recommend pre-marital sex to my future kids, I wouldn't practice it myself."

Is this young woman puritanical, stupid, or out of touch with modern times? Must she feel embarrassed about her celibacy? If not, what can she do with her sexuality? What can she say to herself and others in support of her celibate life-style?

Married woman: "I really think that celibacy is a purer form of life. A celibate has fewer distractions and demands than a married person. Having no spouse and children can give you more freedom to do other things. Not only that, celibacy is 'purer' because to live a meaningful life is placed in your hands."

Celibate man: "I see what you mean, and there's truth in what you say. But it's easy for you—a married person—to say that. You have a husband and children to support you. Think of going home to an empty house. There's no one there to say hello, no one to share the day's problems with, no one to hug you. If a married person has a rough day, he or she can at least talk to someone, or be comforted. There's someone at home to listen and help. I realize that most married people have a lot of problems, and that I have considerable freedom as a celibate. Still, I'm alone."

Married woman: "Perhaps. I still say you have more opportunities; you have more time to do what you want. I know being alone can be painful, but it has its benefits, too. Besides married people are not always together. How do you think it feels to be alone and lonely when you're with someone? And there are times when I just want some rest and free time to be alone and to do what I want to do, but it's almost impossible."

Celibate man: "Don't forget sex. That's something I don't have, and it can solve a lot of problems."

Married woman: "What do you mean? Sex doesn't solve anything. If my husband and I are having problems, sex is the last think I want. If sex solved problems, most people would be happy. If it were only that simple. Having sex when there are problems only causes more problems."

Celibate man: "I'm not talking about mere physical sex. Indeed, sex involves more than the physical. There should be some feeling or care. But, partners should always be available to each other—because love means accepting what you don't like, like having sex even when you don't want to, sex can heal a lot of hurt."

Married woman: "Just a minute! First of all, I don't like your chauvinistic attitude—that a wife should always be available to her husband. Besides, what's wrong with hurting? Sometimes pain is necessary to improve a marriage. For me, such sex would be a way of running from and not resolving problems."

Celibate man: "Still, I think the care, as little as it might be, would help. You have to admit that marriage is easier. You do have sex, and that beats loneliness. Sure, I admit that mere physical sex is like masturbation, but it doesn't have to be that way."

Married woman: "No, I don't admit that marriage is easier. Once again, there's a lot of aloneness and loneliness in marriage, along with the many problems. To see sex as a panacea is a sexist and celibate fiction. Sex is only a part of marriage, and it can't go well unless the other parts are good too."

Celibate man: "I agree that sex is only a part of life, but it can make a big difference. It's bound to draw you out of your lonely aloneness. Do you want to switch places?"

Married woman: "No, thank you. I chose to be married. Do you want to switch?"

Celibate man: "I don't know."

This married woman has chosen and is basically happy with her married life, but she feels that celibacy can be a meaningful alternative. She disagrees with some of the celibate's views on sex, which she judges to be sincere, though sexist, naïve, and even magical. She enjoys sex but thinks that he overestimates its importance. She hints that marriage includes a kind of celibacy and that other issues are more important than sex.

The celibate man, on the other hand, thinks that celibacy and marriage have little in common. He values marriage over celibacy but is uncertain if he would prefer to be married. He seems caught between his frustration and freedom. Interestingly, this celibate regards sex as a healing power that can solve problems and alleviate loneliness.

Now let us listen to the comments of some married people.

"It seems like a thousand years ago when we met. Actually, we were eighteen when we seemed to be so much in love, and felt that everything was possible and nothing could stop us. Now, twenty years later, nothing seems possible. Where has our love gone?

"When we got married, we never wanted to separate. We couldn't stand being without each other. Now, we are like strangers who happen to live at the same place. We can't or don't get close to each other. I thought I felt lonely before I got married; nothing beats this—being lonely and even alone when you're living with someone. When the kids were still young, I didn't notice what was happening. Well, it's happening.

"I feel like I've always been taken for granted. I'm expected to do this, that, whatever, and no one seems to notice. Do they think that everything gets done by magic? They don't realize how boring and demeaning my life can be. What would happen if I didn't cook? What would happen if I didn't slave for a day and a half to cook a thanksgiving meal—a meal I have to schedule in between football games? To say the least, I'm angry.

"More important is that I—I—am taken for granted, expected to give, and always be there, but receive little respect and appreciation in return. Sex is a fiasco. Irony? Although I feel more sexual than ever before, we engage in sex less than before. We have sex when it fits my husband's schedule, which isn't very often. And sex with him is seldom fulfilling. I often end up more tense and frustrated. How do you think it feels to be lonelier after having sex? Sometimes I wonder if I'm worth anything to anyone. I'm tempted to find out."

This woman originally felt that marriage was the way to happiness. Now she feels empty, harried, lonely, and alone. She feels like a function rather than a person. Her spirit is exhausted and starved. She feels exploited, as one used to satisfy the needs of others She wants appreciation, concern, and love. She wonders if she might find it elsewhere.

"I am frustrated, angry, and fed up with sex. After twelve years of marriage, you would think my husband and I would be closer. Instead, we seem farther apart. We seem only to function with each other. We have become friendly strangers.

"His obtuseness amazes me. He doesn't even understand why I refuse to go to bed with him. This may sound selfish, but I want to be Number One, not a poor second to work, newspaper, television, and golf. Is this too much to ask? And when he does try to share himself, which is rare, he's so hesitant and inept. What is he afraid of? I'm not going to kill him.

"I feel like a service station where people stop to refuel and then drive away; I give and give, but get little appreciation and love in return. My husband says that he loves me, but he seldom shows it. He doesn't seem to understand what I want. We have so little common ground. He says that he's satisfied, that he can't understand why I have so many complaints. Sometimes I doubt myself. But no; I know I'm right.

"It's not easy to live with someone who is in his own world—a world he seldom shares. Sure, I enjoy sex, but I'm not going to give myself in the bedroom if my husband does not share in the family room. I can't understand how he does it. I feel used. I only want consistent affection and sharing. Is that asking for too much?"

This woman reflects the feelings and concerns of many women. She feels taken for granted, frustrated, and angry. She feels her dignity and integrity are violated when she engages in genital sex without loving in other ways as well. She wants to be the center of her husband's concern, to be shown love consistently and concretely.

"I hate to admit it, but I'm terribly scared of being impotent. That's one problem I never thought I'd have. I simply can't perform the way I used to. Worse yet, I seldom have the desire to have sex. I get the feeling my wife expects more and is disappointed with me. God, how I hate to go on vacations with her. I don't know what to do with her. And look, I'm forty-four; I'm not old yet, or am I? I feel so tired, and there's always something else to do. I wonder how my wife feels about it? I guess we should talk.

"Why kid myself? We haven't really talked for years. I wouldn't know what to say. I feel so afraid and helpless. Yet, something should be done. Marriage has to be more than a tense adjustment, a keeping out of each other's way. I really try, but my efforts seem so inadequate. Hell, I was happier when I was single. I was by myself—and sure, I felt lonely, but I wasn't so miserable and alone."

This man wants to be intimate, but is afraid. He wonders how he can communicate. He feels vulnerable and inadequate. He dreads what he wants most: love. He wonders if being single would be better than his marital charades. Like the women, his spirit suffers.

Here is another man's story. "Honestly, I really do try, but it seems I'm not good enough. After thirty-six years of marriage, my wife complains more than ever. Her main criticism is that I don't share my feelings, that I really don't say what I think and feel. But when I do try to share, she criticizes me. Then, of course, I withdraw. Wouldn't you?

"Besides, men aren't exactly taught to share; in fact, it's often the opposite. I don't mean to use this as an excuse, but it's true. You know, most males are highly influenced by their mothers—women. And I know that my dad was not the best role model in this respect. My point is why can't women help instead of criticizing?

"Why do women always have to bring up things from the past? Good grief, my wife talks about things that happened twenty years ago as if they happened yesterday. It seems that she has to process everything to death. Why can't she just let the past be in the past, or at least put it on the shelf for awhile? I'm sick and tired of talking things out. Give me a break."

This man echoes the thoughts and feelings of many men. He perceives himself as trapped between pressure to share and criticism for not meeting his wife's expectations. Besides being frustrated, he feels confused and angry about his wife's (woman's?) and his (man's?) approaches. His spirit, too, is drained.

All marriages are not sad. Consider this man's experiences. "After thirty-five years of marriage, I can say that my wife and I enjoy living together more than ever. I love and respect my wife, believe in her, and like her. I am grateful that she puts up with a bozo like me. I guess we are two funny people in love. That's good to say, but when I tell people I am happily married, they look at me as if I'm giving them a line.

"Oh yes, we have had our rough times—with each other and with the kids. But somehow we grew stronger and closer through our difficult times. I couldn't see this at the time it was happening, but in looking back I can see we have become better persons. Speaking for myself, I found it difficult to learn to share my feelings and to take time to listen. But I learned, and I'm a better man for it.

"Sex? It's better than ever. How about that! We don't do it as often as when we were young, but our relationship both in and out of sex is more fulfilling and satisfying. We are closer. Since the kids are out of the house, we have more opportunity just to be with each other. It's like when we were first married, only better."

In the following chapters, single, celibate, and marital lives will be presented as distinct life-forms which call for similar and different modes of sexual behavior. Contrary to popular opinion, being celibate or single do not mean being nonsexual or asexual, but rather being sexual in a way that differs from marital sexuality. We will see how and why, vowed celibate and single persons can and should be sexual in all ways except the way of genital gratification. And married persons can and should be celibate with all people except with their spouses. In whatever we choose to shape our life and direct our sexuality, we are together in our search for healthy intimacy.

Chapter Two
The Sexual Person

How we understand personality, sexuality, and health highly influences the way we feel about, judge, and act on sexuality. For instance, people who hold that sex is merely physical, that one sex is superior to the other, that our behavior has no effect on others, or that celibates art asexual will behave differently than those who believe that sex is wholistic, that males and females are equal and complementary, that our actions have an impact on others, and that celibates are sexual persons. Since it is so important to be aware of our views both theoretically and experientially, let us consider what it means to be sexual, human, and healthy. These discussions will serve as the framework for the remainder of the book.   .

SEX AND SEXUALITY

Sex is understood as conditions of embodiment that predispose and co-determine how we relate to objects, events, and persons. As its etymology indicates (from the Latin *secare*, to cut), sex is relational. Being a man or a woman, which is due to both nature (sex) and nurture (gender), co-determines the way we relate to self, others, and reality in general.

Because we are *embodied* selves, we are sexual. That is not to say that anatomy is destiny, but rather that our embodiment co-constitutes our way of being sexual. Embodiment means that we manifest ourselves and interact with one another in a sexual way—primarily as a man or a woman. Let us reflect on this phenomenology of embodiment more closely.

Our body/sexuality is not something we simply *have* or possess, but is an essential part of who and what we *are*. Embodiment is actually a mode of being. You are your body/sexuality, and your body/sexuality is you. When someone looks at or comments on your body, they look at or comment on you—on your person. When someone treats you as a sex object or just a body, he or she insults and degrades you. When your body changes, you change. These statements may sound simple or complex, but they can be forgotten in daily living. We can forget that we *are* sexually embodied people.

Many western thinkers, teachers, and practitioners have assumed that the body is secondary, that the soul, spirit, psyche, or mind is what is really human or primary. They have reasoned that our bodies were mere containers for the "deeper" realities. Although we may want to understand this truth: "We are our bodies," many attitudes and expressions betray a tendency to see our bodies as things we possess to contain the spirit, or as objects to observe, to use, or to treat. Many scientists, biologists, and physicians, have reinforced this cartesian dualism tendency. When we view ourselves—our (sexual) bodies—as secondary or as objects, we can find it hard to express, to appreciate, to enjoy, and to celebrate our (sexual) bodies/selves.

For instance, a woman's menstrual process is not simply a physiological fact; it is an experiential phenomenon. Although increasingly more women (and some men) are aware of the biochemical impact of menstruation, the menstrual cycle is primarily experiential. Since a woman has and is her body, her menstrual cycle influences the way she experiences reality. Many women, for instance, experience a cyclic change in mood and attitude. This is not to say that a woman is determined by her menstrual cycle; she can choose her attitude and response toward her experience. In short, the menstrual process is a bodily experience that women simply do not have as if they possess a thing; it is an experience that they are.

Embodiment also means that a person's sociality is in some way sexual. Embodiment makes us humanly manifest—accessible and available to others—as men or as women. To see, hear, touch, yearn for, think about, speak to, or relate in whatever way to another involves embodiment, and in this sense are sexual acts. Since sexuality is relational and therefore social, sexuality is never exclusively a private affair. Sexuality is a social reality, and sociality is sexual.

Technically, sex indicates a relatively static dimension of personhood, confined to the conditions which define the differentiations of the sexes. Sex refers to our inheritance, which gives us the possibility and necessity of being sexual. Nature, however, is meaningless without nurture, and potentially is static without learning. How our sex is actualized is contingent on both inheritance and environment. The actualization of sex and gender can be called sexuality.

"Sex" does not exist except in a corpse. Real sex is alive sex, or sexuality. We experience sex, have sex, make sex, express sex, cope with sex, use sex, enjoy sex, celebrate sex, are sexual. Sexuality, in contrast to sex, points to a more dynamic aspect of personhood: to the interaction of sex and gender. Thus, sexuality or how we are sexual is contingent on sex and just as much or more on how we learn to be male and female.

Femininity and masculinity are parts of sexuality. Consider femininity as the way a woman has learned to manifest her sex, or how a woman has learned certain sex roles within a particular culture. Femininity represents learned and sanctioned ways of being a woman. For instance being feminine is associated in most cultures with qualities like sensitivity, intuition, receptivity, nourishment, processing, connection, and care. Likewise, masculinity connotes that a man learns certain social ways to be sexual. In the United States and elsewhere, this is expressed in qualities like objectivity, logic, activity, management, problem solving, detachment, and power. Although emphasis is placed on cultural learning, masculinity and femininity also includes sex or inherited factors. For instance, genetics, biochemistry, physiology, the brain, and so on influence masculinity and femininity. We will see, however, that a woman must incorporate so-called masculine qualities and a man must realize so-called feminine qualities in order to be healthy.

Thus, being male or female—being sexual—is considered to be both a function of inheritance and learning. How a person is sexual is determined by his or her inheritance, by the environment and society/culture, and by the person's attitude. Sexuality should not be reduced to a biological or learned entity.

In light of clinical and empirical evidence, both men and women are considered to be androgynous: Within every man there is a woman, and within every woman there is a man. Although the sexes are distinct, they are not separate. A phenomenology of sexual experience indicates that a man and a woman experience something similar and foreign in each other, and that one sex is the challenging complement of the other sex. In Jungian terms, a man encounters and projects his *anima* and a woman her *animus* upon the other sex. Ideally, each sex should complement each other—men and women helping the other rather than one dominating each other. Such complementary growth is possible and necessary because all people are androgynous. From a Taoist perspective, both ying and yang desire and are incomplete without each other. Male without female and female without male ultimately cease to exist.

Thus, being a woman means that a person is a member of the female sex that incorporates male sexuality. It can be said that a woman's femaleness is primarily in the foreground and her maleness in the background. Likewise, being a man means that a person belongs to the male sex which incorporates female sexuality. The *anima* and *animus* are biological, psychological, social, cultural, and spiritual forces.

DIMENSIONS OF PERSONHOOD

All of us have views about the what it means to be a healthy and ethical human being – and, they highly influence the way we judge, feel about, and behave with ourselves and others. For example, when we exclude the spiritual dimension, we construe sexual experiences radically different from when we include it. In this book, human beings are seen in four fundamental ways and combinations thereof: physically, psychosocially, spiritually, and aesthetically.

The *physical* dimension points to our embodied-incarnated self. Though none of us are ever exclusively physical, we act in certain ways when most of our energy is invested in our pre-rational, physical self. The body demands immediate satisfaction—pleasure, comfort, a reduction of tension or pain. When we experience urgent bodily need, we cannot wait;

postponement of satisfaction makes little sense. We are "a needy me" — prone to act impulsively, without thinking of consequences to self and others. When we try to exist in an exclusively physical way, we want our needs satisfied regardless of anything or anybody.

For instance, an infant is a bodily self who craves immediate satisfaction. Such narcissism is healthy for infants, but when adults act in this way, they manifest regressive or less than healthy behavior: For example, an adult desperately in need of food may lose all respect for self and others and act impulsively to gain immediate satisfaction. When adults maximize the physical dimension of sex, they see others (and themselves) simply somebody to satisfy them.

A centripetal force permeates the physical self. As bodies, we draw reality into us, desiring to taste, touch, feel, hear, and see reality, to be intimate with what is outside but related to our bodies. The senses take in the surroundings so that when one of them is impaired, we are disabled. Our limited perception challenges us to compensate and cope.

Our bodies also insert us in the world as manifest and touchable people. With, through, and in our bodies we connect with others. Because we are incarnated, we are seen, heard, tasted, smelled, and felt. We are vulnerable and therefore, can be hurt—and, helped. Without our bodies, we would be invisible and inviolable.

The *functional* dimension refers to ego activities that are centered around task-oriented behavior, coping mechanisms, and cognitive-rational operations. Functionality describes how we function, the means we take to achieve our goals. As rational beings, we cope with situations, we analyze them, and decide how to act. People who cannot deal with their feelings and thoughts, people, and demands are deemed dysfunctional, or incompetent, and even mentally ill.

Functioning normally involves coping and adjusting, maintaining ourselves, and having adequate control of our lives. When we invest too much in our functional self, we can become so objective and task-oriented that we lack affective sensitivity, intimacy, and spiritual sensibility. We can live from the neck up, and in a sense be "out of our minds."

Most theories of personality and treatment deal with the dimensions of the physical (id, needs, affectivity, satisfaction) and the rational (ego, cognition, volition, coping). However, what is seldom accounted for is the spiritual dimension. Because the spiritual is usually excluded or minimized, we place special emphasis on its role in understanding and dealing with sexuality.

In contrast to our functional ego that deals with life as a series of problems to reflect on and solve, our spiritual self encounters life as a perpetual mystery to suffer and celebrate. Unlike the impersonal detachment of the ego, our spirit seeks personal connection. Both processes are necessary for healthy living. The *spiritual*, however, is paramount because it is transcendent—and, it is paramount in sexuality.

The etymology of transcendence suggests that we seek the more than—the more than the ordinary. In transcendence, we experience the extraordinary in the ordinary; namely, how everything and everyone are interrelated. Metaphorically, we are all different colored, sized, and aged threads of the same tapestry. Individually, many of the threads may not be very functional, attractive, or seemingly worthwhile. Indeed, some threads are strong while others are weak, and some are more beautiful than others. However, when all the threads are woven together, they form an exquisite tapestry. Such a spiritual perspective differs radically from those of the body and ego.

Transcendence does not suggest that we go out of this world; rather, we go deeper into the world where we experience the unity of objects, events, and persons. The experience of transcendence involves appreciating and responding to the way individual parts of reality are interrelated to form a whole. Clinically, this means all human beings are radically interconnected with one another, that our primary condition is to be in community (spirit). Individuality (ego) is important and essential, but it is secondary to community. Unlike the perspective of the ego's individuality, this spiritual view implies that whatever we do has impact on others. Contemporary physics, chaos and systems theories, and ecology models confirm this paradigm of transcendence.

Spiritual experiences also involve paradox and mystery. Unlike the bifurcating "either-or" process of the functional ego, spiritual dynamics involve the unifying experience of "both-and." Instead of focusing on clear and distinct ideas, spiritual people revere and surrender to mystery—a clearly unclear and inexhaustibly accessible source of meaning and fulfillment. Such spiritual experiences as compassion, wonder, contemplation, and love are neither irrational nor rational; they are transrational. Spiritual, sex incorporates qualities and activities such as care, respect, reverence and, most importantly: love.

Spirit deepens sex, and sex embodies spirit. Sexuality gives spirituality concrete humanness; spirituality gives sexuality lasting vitality. In spiritual genital sexuality, a person can experience an aesthetic unity of concrete sexuality and transcendent spirituality. Indeed healthy spirituality can never be sexless because spirituality is always in some way embodied. Likewise, sexuality is always more or less spiritual because it is inclined toward transcendence—a going beyond individuality toward communion with others and God. God is construed as the uncreated energies of love—the primordial and perpetual source and force of desiring union with one another. God is the Creator, Sustainer, Motivator, and Finality of life.

The *aesthetic* dimension refers to the unity of the physical, rational, and spiritual. In this light, beauty can be considered to be a harmony of matter, form, and transcendent meaning—that is, it is embodied, rational, and spiritual. When we say that a person is beautiful, we mean that he or she lives in harmony, manifesting (embodiment) transcendent meaning (spirituality) with good form (functionality). When we reject or violate any of these dimensions, we are less than whole—or, less than good, healthy, and beautiful.

Aesthetic sex protects and promotes the unity of matter, form, and spiritual meaning. Spiritual (loving) sex is beautiful because it is embodied, and pleasing, has form and style, and incorporates love and spiritual meaning. Our challenge is to seek beautiful and transcendent sex: to experience the union of self and others, to go beyond self to and for each other, and ultimately to experience the presence of God—the source and destiny of perfect unison.

THE SPIRITUALITY OF SEXUALITY

Desires reside deep within the core of our being. Not only do we "have" many desires, we "are" our desires. We are made to yearn for more than we are. The etymology of desire indicates that from the core of our being we long for heaven or perpetual communion. Desires affirm that our existence is to stand out beyond our individual selves, that our existence is co-existence, that to be is to be with. When we no longer desire, we die. Instead of reaching for the stars and, trying to touch the other, we stay within ourselves. Heaven is fulfilled desires; hell is unfulfilled desires.

We desire in many ways: food, shelter, safety, success, control, esteem, validation, and love. Some desires maintain us, while others enhance our life. An increasing amount of empirical evidence indicates that the desire for connection is the most important and essential dynamic for healthy living. In fact, people who go beyond themselves to foster communal growth are more likely to live longer and better than those who isolate or are self-contained individuals.

Sexuality of whatever type is one of the clearest manifestations of this spiritual dynamic to connect beyond ourselves. The desire to go beyond oneself by being intimate with another is sexuality's spiritual dimension. The spiritual energy of connection is always involved in sexuality; it is the life of sex. Sex without any spirit whatsoever is impossible. Sex with little spirit is lust. Thus, physical sex and even sexual abuse involves the spiritual. This is the paramount reason why sexual abuse is unhealthy and heinous because it not only violates our body but moreso our embodied spirit. In short, sexuality is both an embodied and spiritual presence. One without the other is fragmented and less than whole, less than healthy.

Too often, however, spirituality and sexuality are separated. We repress and violate the transcendent—the urge for communion—in our sexuality. Or instead of despiritualizing sexuality, we desexualize spirituality. We try to live spiritual lives while repressing our sexuality,or we consider genital sexuality only a biological function, and consequently degrade human personhood. To repress sexuality while promoting spirituality is similar to repressing spirituality while promoting sexuality;both are unchaste. One approach identifies the human person simply as a rational being; the other makes a person simply a sexual rational being.

In fact, the human person is a unity of physicality, functionality, and spirituality. Nevertheless, mass media and education can give a less than whole picture of sexuality. Consequently, people observe and learn how to practice less than healthy sex.

Sexuality involves infinitely more than pleasure. Sex summons connection, intimacy, harmony, solace, safety, esteem, validation, fun, relief, ecstasy, pleasure, curiosity, control, empowerment, and mystery. The more the spiritual is fostered in sexuality, the more such experiences come alive. The more we respond to both the embodied and spiritual aspects of sexuality, the more are fulfilled and grow. Conversely, the more we forget, repress, dissociate, or numb our spiritual selves in sexuality, the more we are deprived of connection and lasting fulfillment. Sex with little spirit engenders temporary satisfaction rather than ongoing growth.

When sex is turned inward to self, its transcendent movement often results in narcissism, exploitation, and manipulation. Such "sexification" makes oneself and others sex objects, frustrating the desire for lasting connection. Although sex may be pleasurable, its spirit is forgotten, alienated, and violated. As members of sexaholics anonymous would say, the desire for God (Spirit) is displaced with lustful sex. Conversely, healthy sex can motivate us to be closer to the Divine in ourselves and in others—in us.

HEALTHY, GOOD, NORMAL, MAD AND BAD

People often look at sex as either healthy or unhealthy, and mistakenly assume that if their sexual behavior is not unhealthy, then it is healthy. However, an absence of pathology does not equal health. If so, then what is healthy sex? Unhealthy sex? Are healthy and normal the same? Let us be clear about what is healthy, good, normal, mad, and bad sexuality.

Healthy sexuality is congruent with and fosters wholistic growth. Instead of living out of repression, fixation, regression, perversion, disintegration, or any psychopathology, healthy persons grow in wholeness and promote the welfare of self and others. The essential dynamic in healthy sex is committed and viable love without psychopathology and immaturity. Healthy sex is good and beautiful because it promotes the appreciation and nourishment of our physicality, functionality, and spirituality.

In our approach, a key variable is *normal* sexuality. Normality simply means that we can maintain, ourselves, cope with everyday demands and behave within the norms of society and mental health. Normal persons have a grip on life, can satisfy their basic needs, and lack pathology. Still, they are not necessarily healthy. A prevention of psychopathology is part of being healthy but does not totally constitute health. Normal sexuality means that we can cope with and effectively satisfy our sexual needs without behaving abnormally. In reducing sexual tension, we maintain ourselves but do not necessarily promote healthy and holy growth. Sexual behavior is often normal without being pathological or healthy.

Madness characterizes those who are closed to experiences significant to and necessary for healthy (wholistic) growth. From the perspective, normal people, not just abnormal people, can be alienated from experiences vital to healthy and happy living, and in this sense be "mad." In such "normal madness", we function within the confines of normal society and do not manifest pathological symptoms; nonetheless, we are closed to realities necessary for healthy living. For instance, workaholics, maximize task-oriented success and minimize other essential experiences like love, play, and compassion; consequently, they are normal but more or less mad. They live less than wholistic lives because they forget or repress their spiritual dimensions. Many kinds of sexual activity are normal and not pathological but are more or less mad. For example, genital behavior that only reduces tension and does not promote individual and communal growth is normal and mad, neither unhealthy nor healthy.

Mad sex usually lacks such qualities as mindfulness, care, responsibility, respect, and love. Some mad sex is unhealthy (e.g., pedophilia and rape); other sexual behavior, though not abnormally mad or socially punished, is normally mad. For instance, treating another as a sex object is normal, is usually tolerated, and is not treated as sick or criminal. Nevertheless it is mad because it violates the whole person, especially one's spiritual dimension.

Sexual behavior can also be considered in light of goodness and badness. In our psycho-spiritual framework, *goodness* refers to behavior that is congruent with and fosters healthy love, to behavior that promotes the welfare of community: self, others, and God. Etymologically, the good refers to what fosters togetherness, harmony, and peace. Conversely *badness* refers to the violation or destruction of communal growth and welfare. The good enlightens and unifies us; the bad darkens and separates us.

We can see that goodness/badness and healthy/non-healthy can be related and can be quite different. For instance, although neurotic and psychotic persons are unhealthy, they can be good, for they may conscientiously strive to promote love and spiritual growth of self and others .

Some people are sick saints. Other sick persons, however, may intentionally and consistently live a life of vice rather than virtue. On the other hand, normal persons who are not unhealthy in the traditional sense can still be bad. Although these people are adjusted and lack pathology, they fail to live according to the spiritual dictums of life.

Differentiating between being mad and being bad, between symptom and sin, is difficult but important especially in the areas of law and morality. One fundamental difference between them is an individual's level of intentionality. Mad persons seldom consciously or intentionally promote madness; usually psychological and/or organic processes motivate them. In contrast to mad people, bad people are more intentional and exercise more choice in what they do. Nevertheless, mad persons can choose to be bad. Where one is on the continuum of choice is a key differentiating factor between sickness and sin or crime. Indeed, most of us are sometimes mad or bad, and our degree and frequency of madness and badness reflect our lack of healthiness and holiness.

Truly healthy persons are at least implicitly good because they promote communal growth and harmony. To be sure, healthy persons are capable of and can perform bad acts, but basically their lives are good. Their paramount value is to live a virtuous life. Normal persons who lead consistently good (virtuous) lives are healthy.

In short, healthy sexuality includes an on-going integration of the sexual and spiritual. Sexuality vitalizes, concretizes, and incarnates the spiritual; spirituality nourishes, deepens, and transcends sexuality. But when we bifurcate sexuality and spirituality, we identify ourselves and others simply as sexual or spiritual beings; consequently, we are less than whole and therefore mad. Those who practice mere physical sex may achieve conversely, pleasurable satisfaction and temporary fulfillment, but they experienced little spiritual joy, depth, and permanency. Sexless people become disembodied, dry, lifeless, and mad. They become either cerebral robots or untouchable spirits.

The ideal is to experience, not simply talk about, the lived unity of spirituality and sexuality. The challenge is to embody and manifest spirit in sex. Healthy and holy people witness to this unity of sexuality and spirituality.

In the next three chapters, we will describe and analyze primary, affective, and genital sexuality in their physical, functional, spiritual, and aesthetic dimensions. We will show how they can be healthy, good, mad, or bad. A primary thesis is that when sexuality, functionality, and spirituality are integrated, sexuality is good, beautiful, healthy, and holy.

CHAPTER THREE
PRIMARY SEXUALITY

Considerable research exists on how men and women think, process, judge, feel, manage, communicate, and in general experience life. Empirical and clinical data have shown that men and women are similar and different. Popular books have helped us to understand that men are from Mars and women are from Venus and that women speak in a different voice. This chapter explores how and why men and women are different, equal, and complimentary as well as how they can challenge and help each other to be better men and women.

FEMALE AND MALE EXISTENCE

Primary sexuality refers to how men and women are present to and interact with oneself, others, to reality in general, and to God. Based on phenomenological and other research, one proposition is that women tend to interweave their experience, and men tend to differentiate their experience. Due to innate and environmental factors, women move relatively more toward wholeness, internalization, and concrete care, while men move toward categorization, externalization, and abstract principles. Women's experiences are prone more than men's to seek an integral and centralized process, while men's experiences are more prone to be compartmentalized. A woman experiences reality as a network of many factors (objects, events, and persons) that she cares for; a man is more likely to cope with the individual parts of reality. To be sure, these propensities are not mutually exclusive. Because we are (by nature and nurture) androgynous, we can and do, more or less, actualize both sexual potentials. The challenge is to actualize both while remaining true to one's primary sexual identify.

Consider the case of married couple who have been tense and aggressive toward each other throughout the day and have not reconciled. The woman will usually be less inclined than the man to be intimate that particular night. The man, however, can more easily differentiate his experiences; in this case: the troublesome day and the intimate encounter. She is not as inclined to compartmentalize her experiences. When the husband expects his wife to put the day aside and make love, she is likely to look at him as if he is out of his mind and think, "How can he even consider being intimate when the day has been so miserable? Does he think I can push a button to turn the day off? If we can't make love outside the bedroom, we're not going to make it in the bedroom. What does he think I am—a robot?" The husband thinks, "What's wrong with her? So we had a rough day—does that mean we shouldn't have sex? Why can't she just forget about the day and have sex at night?"

The perception and judgment of both the husband and wife have assets and deficits. The woman is right: Genital intimacy should not be something one disassociates from the rest of the day; intimacy should be integrated with and an affirmation of an on-going intimacy. Sexual intimacy without other forms of intimacy can be experienced as exploitation and phony—a kind of prostitution. Sexual activity can easily serve as a cover and an anesthetic for underlying problems.

However, the man's sensibility is not meaningless; to suppress or to put things on the shelf for awhile can engender reconciliation as well as an enjoyable time. If every problem had to be worked out before intimacy could occur, intimacy would be greatly curtailed. Nevertheless, to frequently minimize or repress problems will sooner or later harm sexual intimacy and perhaps destroy the overall relationship.

Women more often than men strive to unify sex and love. For instance, when a woman wants to be sexually involved with a man, she usually seeks a sign of love. Although such a request can be linked to deficiencies like a need for approval, her integrative propensity still encourages her to look for love in sex. To be sure, a woman can separate sex and love, but a man usually separates them more readily. Similarly, although a woman can be intimately involved with more than one man at a time, she rarely engages in such multi-involvements. A man, however, can live separate lives more easily. A "family man"—an apparently good husband and father—can periodically engage a prostitute or have an affair. A woman can also behave promiscuously, but she is less likely to do so not only because of social factors but also because of her primary sexuality.

It is as if such men can put women in separate categories. Leaving one woman, a man can put her aside and later be intimate with another—sometimes in a seemingly genuine way. A woman, on the other hand, has more difficulty in romancing more than one "number one." Two or more men would, it seems, conflict within her personality. Of course, one sex is capable of doing what the other can do. Our contention here, however, is to describe the dynamics of what usually happens.

Again, consider how a man can treat a woman as a sex object—almost exclusively in physical terms. He can disassociate her physical sexuality from the rest of her being, fragmenting the whole woman and concentrating on her physical attributes. Indeed, a woman can also see and treat a man as a sex object, but usually not quite as easily or as often. She is inclined to look for more than one dimension of a man.

Men's differentiated mode of existence explains their tendency to put various experiences in different categories. They involve themselves in one experience while putting others aside, enabling them to be more detached and less intimate with their experience. Their task oriented approach can serve them well in problematic situations—and, it can be detrimental to intimacy.

Since all people are androgynous, women can differentiate experiences and be task-oriented, and men can interweave experiences and be caring. In this sense, a man should actualize the women within him, and a woman the men within her. Men can deepen their appreciation of n how the various parts of experience impact on one another as well as to care for (not just deal with) others. They can seek to promote and realize the"*anima* within themselves. Women can strengthen their ability to differentiate experiences—to realize the *animus* within themselves.

Along with cultural programming and personal expectations , women's integrative, caring style and a men's differentiated, task-oriented style can influence their choice of and performance in work . A female physician, for example, may see and care for patients a little differently than a male physician. And, patients may experience female and male physicians differently. This is not to imply that one sex is better than the other, but rather that a physician of one gender may be better than another for a particular individual. Some women would prefer the one to the other not only because of the physician's competence.

Theoretically, primary sexuality influences any experience. Another example is architects. A female architect might design a building (particularly for women) differently than a man. Because she perceives reality and women from the perspective of a woman, she may conceive a dwelling place that would differ from what a man would conceive. It is possible for architecture or anything else to be primarily male or female. And it is possible that our U.S. architecture, as well as other areas, are one-sidedly male.

Let us probe this example further. If a woman's dwelling place is influenced by her primary sexuality, the architecture, furnishings, art works, and general structure and atmosphere of her home should be congruent with and promote her female experience. It is possible that some men have designed female living conditions that are less than optimum for a woman's comfort and development. Female community structures like convents and dormitories (as well as working areas) are often more linear, staid, functional and "masculine" rather than centered, dynamic, caring, and "feminine." In short, a woman may be more intimately involved with her space. A man, on the other hand, may be more detached from the personal meaning of his space and be focused on its utility. Again, these tendencies are not mutually exclusive.

Time, for example, may be experienced differently. Women may interweave the past and future with the present more than men who are prone to separate them. Thus, when dealing with a present issue, a woman may bring up past events; whereas as man more commonly wants to "forget" about them. For example, it is not unusual for a woman to talk about past experiences as if they recently occurred. Her past is often more present to her, particularly if it involves intimacy. In time, one approach without the other becomes one-sided and increasingly stressful.

Neither the male nor female mode of existence is superior; both are equal and essential. One without the other leads to a fragmented and impoverished life and culture. Furthermore, both Yin and Yang need and desire each other. They are essential and interrelated parts of the Tau or the whole of life. In fact, one without the other violates and eventually destroys life.

Men should realize their female and feminine dimensions in their male and masculine ways, and women should realize their male and masculine dimensions in their female and feminine ways. They become whole but not the same, alike but not identical. Such an androgynous integration of both male-masculine and female-feminine presence is needed for healthy living. To expand and concretize these ideas, let us consider the experience of primary sexuality from four perspectives: physical, functional, spiritual, and aesthetic.

EXPERIENCES OF PRIMARY SEXUALITY

We have seen that our bodies/ourselves influence the way we act and feel. Some sex differences are subtle, like how men and women walk, touch, caress, and nurture. More overt distinctions include behavior like how men and women dress, play sports, work manually, and have sex. Reproductive functions, personal care, and child bearing clearly differentiate the sexes along with their more covert hormonal and brain processes.

How we and society perceive our bodies/ourselves is also linked to primary sexuality. Think of when you judge your body or sex as inferior, you can feel and act inferior. You can be programmed to feel that your body includes certain meanings and excludes others. A woman may see her sexuality primarily as a means of pleasing and being useful to men. She can be conditioned to view her sexual self as an object and function to attract and generate male applause. Of course, concern about personal appearance is healthy, but when it is based on a need to please, self-diminishment, frustration, unhappiness are likely consequences. Unfortunately, mass media and advertisements reinforce this sexist mode of normal madness.

Men, also, can be conditioned to take negative attitudes toward their sexuality. A small man, for instance, may feel inferior because Western culture supports a large and powerful ideal of the male body. Men, however, retain social acceptance when they get out of shape, while women can be pressured to stay "attractive" and "in shape" when in public or on display. For instance, an over-weight woman may encounter more obstacles with job promotions and marital prospects than a man will experience.

When one treats another as a sex object, one focuses on that person as simply "a body" or some being that has a body—"somebody." Such a lack of respect for the whole person is an insult to that person. When treated as a sex object, a person feels degraded and often resentful because he or she is not appreciated as a whole person, but simply as a body to be exploited. The truth is that there is not such entity as "a body," but only a psychospiritual body or an embodied spirit.

With the exception of some biological process, few activities are male or female in themselves. To be sure, both sexes should have equal opportunity to do most of the same activities in complementary ways. Clearly, injustice and problems occur when one sex feels superior, oppresses the other, or tries to be the same as the other sex.

From a functional perspective, it is not so much what men and women do, but how they do it. We have seen that both men and women can care and be task-oriented, but how they implement these activities differ. A house husband's experience of and the way he functions with children and housework may differ from a housewife's experience. A female physician can function as well or better than a man, but how she interacts with her patients and how they experience her differs somewhat from that of a male physician.

Women have been and still are oppressed in career (functional) areas. Instead of being hindered from pursuing certain fields, both women and men should be allowed and encouraged to be slightly different engineers, physicians, mechanics, nurses, and teachers. When girls are depicted in traditionally masculine roles, their chances of pursuing these fields are highly increased. Recently, for instance, more women than men are becoming psychologists.

Remember that being a little girl sets the foundation for being a woman and that being a little boy is the ground from which a man grows. People, especially parents, positively and negatively influence what kind of woman or man a person will be and how he or she will function. In short, one's beginning highly influences one's end. If a woman as a girl could only play in "feminine" ways, her view of being a woman was already being formed to a large degree. If she were allowed to be assertive, and do so-called "masculine" things, she probably would grow up with a different view of being a woman. Fortunately, role models in children's books and mass media have improved for women, and perhaps not as much for men.

Since a woman's cultural and sub-cultural programming highly influences her self-concept and sexual roles, a woman can ask herself certain questions: Did (or does) my mother sell herself short, act like a servant , or take second place to men? Does she take pride in who she is, enjoy doing many things, feel equal to men, and feel free? What is her view of womanhood? Did (and does) she think that women are just as important and contribute as much as men? Did she encourage me to be competent and competitive as well as caring and receptive? How did my father act towards me and my mother? Did (and does) he treat and discourage me to function as well as and to succeed as much as boys? How do my parents treat me now?

A girl may undergo pressures that boys seldom experience. Although some girls may have freedom in childhood to be an individual and to be assertive, they can be pressured in adolescence to subordinate their vocational goals to the finding of a marital partner. Although attitudes are changing, One can still observe the enormous amount of sexism against both sexes in mass media.

Although more focus is presently on women's rights, men have also been oppressed from becoming wholly themselves, perhaps as much or more than women. For instance, many men have been culturally programmed to distrust their feelings of affection and fail to learn how to be wholly intimate. Their self-esteem often depends too much on career success and not nearly enough on concrete and consistent caring. Many men have been conditioned to see themselves as necessarily the main economic provider and often the "head" of home, religion, and society. These and other oppressive scripts frustrate growth within and between men themselves as well as with women.

More specifically, a common problem is that many men never learn to understand and to deal with a woman's anger. Many well-intentioned men avoid or withdraw from female anger, while others attack it. In either approach—flight or fight—men have difficulty listening to women. Perhaps they fear rejection and criticism, are unable to accept conflict, or are afraid of being dominated. Whatever the reason, their inability to deal with angry women aborts communication and engenders more problems both personally and professionally.

A man may also question himself: What kind of role model was (is) my father? Can I be truly affectionate with others? Must I function in so-called masculine ways that exclude spontaneity, gentleness, and care? Can I share feelings and responsibilities with a woman? Can I be a "househusband"? Can I surrender to a woman? How can women help me? Where is the woman in me?

The childhood of men also varies considerably and has a significant impact on their lives. What were (and are) my parents like? Was my dad a phantom father? Did he show affection and enjoy time with me, or did he spend time only when there was a job to be done? Was my mother over-burdened with family responsibilities? How did she treat me? Did I always have to do "masculine" things? Did I learn to see girls as inferior, fickle, and servile, or as domineering and cold? Was I taught that boys hide their fears and pain? How do I see girls or women now? Do I feel free to express my whole self? What is my view of being a true man?

Men often think that the image of a man is much clearer and more set than a woman's. But is it? Is being an authentic man the same as being masculine? Masculinity is highly influenced by cultural programming, yet what is regarded as masculine in one culture is not regarded so in another. Does a true man never cry and feel vulnerable, or rarely shows his love? Is it "unmanly" to cook, to sew, to do housework? What is an "androgynous man"?

Men can be less certain of their identity often because their mother's influence is stronger than that of their fathers. Some fathers seem to be working, on the computer, reading, watching television, or just too busy or too tired to be available. If this is true, a boy's early preparation for being a man may have been quite limited. Parenthetically, the absence of a mature man or father can also be detrimental to the growth of a woman.

Nevertheless, women are often more certain than men of their sexual identity. This may occur because mothers usually spend more time qualitatively and quantitatively with their children; consequently, the mother's attitudes maybe more significant in influencing the kind of a woman the girl will become.

Along with physical and functional dimensions, our *spiritual* self is also sexual. We have seen that there is the strong tendency to bifurcate sexuality and spirituality. Indeed, sexuality has often been despiritualized, and spirituality has often been desexualized. However, both sexuality and spirituality are essential and interrelated dimensions of being human. A sexual person—male or female—is spiritual. Spirituality without sexuality dehumanizes the person.

Personal history and cultural programming can also have a decisive impact on sexual/spiritual growth. For example, if a boy learns that spiritual experience is unimportant, feminine, or secondary to functional achievement and success, he will have little incentive for spiritual growth. Men, including clergy, can legislate and administrate matters regarding spirituality, but fail in their spiritual life. If a woman is programmed to take the back seat in spiritual leadership, she can sell herself short and be prevented from making her contribution. Although women have been the spiritual intra structure in religions, they have seldom held public positions of power and leadership. Is this the best way?

Consider some of the more functional, political, and ministerial aspects of religion. It is a particular danger to deal with ministry only or primarily according to male models. The ministry and leadership of women in religious and spiritual domains are sometimes unnecessarily curtailed. Women are "allowed" to promote spirituality and to have positions of authority in "their own" domains, but they could be given more opportunities for the benefit of both sexes. Indeed, women are entering various areas of spiritual ministry in greater numbers; one can hope this will be encouraged to continue.

Other spiritual issues can be reconsidered in light of primary sexuality. For instance, do men and women pray differently? Do they conduct and experience liturgy differently? Perhaps men and women experience and articulate spirituality in different but complementary ways. Important differences may exist.

Men often direct and control, at least externally, the spiritual lives of women. Are there dangers when men have more overt power in directing women's spirituality? Certainly, men can help women's spiritual formation, but women may direct women (and men) differently. Furthermore, men may be constricted when they only have access to "male spirituality". Surely, it is better to have a choice.

Until recently, men had more and better formal religious education than women. For example, a nun was seldom educated better than a priest, but now many religious and lay women have acquired higher education. Kept out of traditional centers of religious education, such as seminaries, women went to universities. These "naïve, second class" women often got as good or better education then men. Furthermore, since they were in a heterosexual environment as contrasted with a homosocial environment, they had more concrete and constructive opportunities to cope with celibate heterosexuality. Perhaps the intellectual and sexual power of women intimidates men. Perhaps women's education, criticism, creativity, and heterosexual adjustment threaten some men to the extent they must keep women in second place.

Although women comprise a majority portion of the spiritual infrastructure, seldom do they have superstructure positions of authority and opportunity. What would happen if men shared their power and responsibility, listened to and learned from women, and worked and prayed equally together? What would happen if women had more explicit influence in forming religious structures, guidelines, and policies? If there were more female input, it is likely that different decisions would have been made in regards to clerical sex abuse.

Love, the paramount dynamic of spirituality, can also be considered in light of primary sexuality. Do men and women love differently? We have seen that men are tend separate love from other experiences and women are more likely to integrate them. Women are inclined to value and promote care more than principle, and experience more than theory. Women's integral presence and tendency to promote love can be a positive and powerful influence on individual and communal spirituality. Unfortunately, some women minimize their own powerful presence and instead seek the questionable power of men. They try to follow a male model while minimizing or forgetting the essence of spirituality: love.

Perhaps the male propensity to be task-oriented has predisposed men to maximize the value of religious administration, legislation, problem solving, and rational theology, thus minimizing spiritual sensibility and experience. It seems that men can be more easily programmed to pursue rational and theoretical knowledge, forgetting transrational experience. To talk about and administer religion differs from fostering spiritual living.

Finally, let us consider aesthetically beautiful/ sexual people. They may be old, physically unattractive, and functionally impaired. Yet, they are beautiful because their spirit speaks and is in harmony with their embodied selves. Old persons can be sexually beautiful because they embody the spirit of life. Crippled and deformed persons—men and women of integrity— can radiate their dignity and wisdom. The arthritic hands of an aging, healthy, and holy woman or man are more beautiful than the twenty year old's sensuous hands. The old hands tell a life story. They speak of joy and suffering, of intimacy and aloneness, of pleasure and pain, of good and evil, of success and failure, of you and me. They embody the spirit of everyone. They are beautiful.

People who experience life aesthetically are at least implicitly in contact with the spiritual. However, a difference between the aesthetic and the spiritual is that the accent of beauty is on the dynamic whole, while spirituality focuses on the spirit of that whole. In short, aesthetic experience can foster spirituality and vice versa. It is not accidental that places of sacred worship usually incorporate symbols of beauty—objects like paintings and activities like singing which can foster spiritual experiences.

To summarize: People are primarily male or female androgynous beings. This primary sexuality is experienced and manifested in physical, functional, spiritual, and aesthetic ways, and in combinations of these dimensions. Our challenge is to become whole sexual selves, to foster the optimum conditions that promote androgynous, sexual, functional, and spiritual growth.

CHAPTER FOUR
AFFECTIVE SEXUALITY

We have seen that all human activity is sexual insofar as we are men and women. Sexuality influences the way we perceive, think, judge, feel, act, and interact. In short, our sex impacts on how we work, play, suffer, and enjoy – how we live. Out of this primary sexuality emerges another mode of sexuality: affective sexuality—the dimension of interpersonal intimacy.

Affective sexuality refers to feelings, modes, and emotion ("affects") that move toward or incorporate intimacy. It describes how we are affectively (more than cognitively) motivated to become closer to one another—to "touch" physically, functionally, spiritually, and aesthetically. We feel "affection" for another; we desire to be closer to another.

In affective sexuality, a key word is "intimacy,"—the experience of self-disclosure and sharing. We want to show and share ourselves as well as to see and receive the other. Intimacy may be primarily physical without any long term care or commitment, or it may involve deeper and lasting dimensions of our spiritual self. We can be "turned on," "tuned in," or involved for moments, hours, months, years, or a lifetime. Whatever the case, we yearn, desire, want, and need to be close to others.

Affective sexuality can take many forms. Depending on our intentions, feelings, and opportunities, our "feelings for" someone may motivate us to disclose and share ourselves in the close, permanent union of marital love or friendship, or it may be less affective and intimate as in a gracious meeting or a warm recognition.

An important distinction is that affective intimacy can be an end in itself, or it can be in service and part of genital behavior. For instance, a warm smile or a respectful caress can be an end in itself, or it may lead to or be part of a genital experience. Affective sexuality can stand on its own as a way of relating to another person, or it can be a prelude to genital activity. The failure to make this distinction can make for unnecessary and serious problems. When affective and genital sexuality are confused or when affection is seen as necessarily leading to genital sex, frustration confusion, and violence are among the many possible consequences.

The primary way to determine if affection is an end in itself or a means to genital sex is to examine our motives. Motivations are conscious and unconscious, in both self and other. I can be in conflict with my own intentions, or my intentions may conflict with yours, or vice versa. For example, I may sincerely intend to be only affectionate with you but find myself being genitally aroused. Or, you may be intimate with me without any genital desires, but I may become genitally aroused, or I may misinterpret your affection as an invitation to genital sex. One of us may find ourselves in a (genital) situation that neither intended nor desired. The challenge is to be aware of one's own as well as the other's intentions.

When affective sexuality leads to genitality in self, other, or both, we can affirm the presence of genital sex and freely choose what course of action to take. A negative approach is to be unaware of or be at odds with these feelings. Conversely, when we are more open to the possibility of genital sex in affective encounters, we are freer to pursue genital sex or to promote affective sexuality in itself.

EXPERIENCES OF AFFECTIVE SEXUALITY

Reflect on sexuality in its aesthetic dimension. Such "affective aesthetic" sexuality incorporates both affective and aesthetic components so that feelings of intimacy are permeated with beauty. Consider a ballet that manifests the erotic and aesthetic: The performers show affection and aesthetic intimacy. Their dance is an end in itself; the dancers have no intention of using their dance as a means to genital sexuality. If their dance were to be used as a prelude to genital intimacy, it would take on a different tone and flavor. The dancers' intentions are to express and celebrate erotic and aesthetic intimacy solely as an end in itself.

On an everyday level, consider a man and a woman who dance with each other on an affective aesthetic plane. Although their dancing may not be objectively very aesthetic, they feel beautiful while becoming affectively intimate with each other. Their dancing can be an end in itself, or it can be an overture to genital relations. For instance, a married couple may dance in an erotic-aesthetic way as a prelude to genitality, while two friends enjoy their dance without genital intentions.

Indeed, problems can emerge when partners have different motivations, like when a woman understands a dance as an end in itself but her partner uses it as an avenue to genital sex. Using the dance as a means, the man will probably become genitally aroused. Like many women, she may sense such intentions and choose to cooperate with or impede them, or if she is unaware of his intentions, she may be surprised as his intentions become more overt.

Another possibility is that a woman (or a man) may misinterpret a man's (woman's) intentions, thinking that affection will lead to a date or spending more time together. If the man has no such intentions, the woman may feel confused, hurt, frustrated, or angry when he avoids more intimacy. Although the man may be innocent, he could be aware of the woman's mood and intentions, and she of his. To prevent frustration, exploitation, or other pain, ideally both partners should know their own and the other's intentions.

Still another example is a couple who intend their affective behavior to be an end in itself but unintentionally become genitally aroused. If they deny their arousal state, they may feel conflicted and perhaps guilty. On the other hand, they might step back (physically, psychologically, and spiritually) and take stock of their situation. They can decide to promote genital feelings, or suppress, sublimate, or integrate them, and throttle their affective dialogue. It is possible for a man and a woman to be chaste and celibate lovers, if they communicate their motives.

Another couple may engage in deep care and self-revelation. The man may interpret this affective encounter as a step toward genital gratification, whereas the woman may see it as the beginning of a more consistent and longer lasting relationship. One of them will be disappointed and perhaps hurt. Because the man openly and personally shares himself, it is understandable that the woman assumes a promise for a future relationship. If, his intentions do not included such a promise, the woman, is likely to the become confused, frustrated, and angry when he does not meet her expectations. Ideally, the man can realize that such behavior can be misinterpreted and make his intentions clear. The woman can become more assertive and proclaim her feelings and intentions.

Similar problems can exist in marriage. One partner may want to be physically affectionate with genital sex ,and the other partner intimate without it. Women particularly like to embrace and to be physically intimate as a way of expressing love. Such intimacy is highly sexual though not explicitly genital, and too often men misinterpret this affection as a desire for genital sex. When a woman thwarts the man's advances toward genital expression, both become frustrated, hurt, and angry. The key point here is that all physical affection need not and should not lead to genital behavior. A couple who hold and caress each other can have an intimate, pleasurable, and loving experience that need not lead to genital behavior.

An unnecessary problem arises because western males are often seen as the bearers of genital sexuality and Western women as the guardians of affective sexuality. People in the United States usually consider erotic-aesthetic behavior as feminine and therefore natural for women. However, when a man expresses erotic aesthetic behavior, such as in the performing and fine arts, he may be considered effeminate or unmanly. The premise is that a "man" is defined as affectively aggressive and controlled, not aesthetic. Thus, when he is affectively aesthetic, particularly as an end in itself, he is seldom supported and he may be ridiculed. Indeed, such behavior is sexist..

Most men are strongly prone to use affective sexuality as a means to genital sexuality. When a man expresses affection, he usually desires genital relations as well. Unfortunately, it is difficult for most men to promote and enjoy physical affection without any genital intention.

Too often when a man does express his affection as an end, a woman will often hesitate and wonder about his true intentions. Or if his intentions are pure, both men and women are apt to judge him as sexually repressed, latently homosexual, unmanly, or stupid. To be affectively sexual without genital intentions is more difficult for most men than for most women.

As in the other modes of sexuality, aesthetic and spiritual sexuality are similar and often closely related. A key distinction is based on which dimension—the aesthetic or spiritual—is accented. In spiritual affective sexuality the accent is on spirituality with affective components. For example, the language of some spiritual writers has an affective tone as the following passage illustrates: "My heart burns with love. I desire to be with you, and I yearn to give my all to you, O Lord, my love. I want to embrace you with every fiber of my being and have you embrace me. Though I am unworthy, I am yours forever." Contrast this passage with one that is strongly cognitive. "A knowledge of God, which includes reading scripture, is important in fostering one's spiritual life. If one does not reflect on the articulation of God, on God's Word, one loses an important source of spiritual sustenance and motivation." Affective sexuality another literary example is some sacred scriptures such as the Song of Songs. The poetic passages of this book center primarily around life in love. The song can be considered spiritual poetry that celebrates affective sexuality. Reading this work could be a prelude to genital intimacy, but can also proclaim the joy of intimacy without geniality.

Interpersonal care can be made another mode of spiritual affection. A warm and gentle smile can be an affective expression of care and affirmation. When a son embraces his father, affective sexuality can be present while remaining in service of spiritual gratitude. A comforting touch, a supportive caress, and a compassionate word can express feelings of intimacy that are unlikely to lead to genital arousal. However, physical affection that is highly erotic with little spiritual or aesthetic influence can easily evoke and lead to genital involvement

When their care (or spirit) is forgotten or suppressed physical affection can easily lead to genitally behaviors Behavior like erotic dancing, sensuous touching, and sexually seductive language can readily engender genital arousal. Then, those involved can decide what they will do—promote, express, suppress, limit, stop, sublimate, or integrate genital feelings.

When no care is present or intended, physical affective sexuality is mad or bad. In this case, physicality is separated from functionality and spirituality. People treat each other as sex objects, as merely physical beings to satisfy their physical needs. To reiterate, this dissociative process is neither healthy nor good, for people are infinitely more than physical. Speech and flirting that exclude respectful care, activities like dancing that focus entirely on physical arousal, or modes of dress that maximize eroticism and immodesty, only promote dis-integration. These and other forms of affective sexuality can promote genital sex without care. Even if such activities do not culminate in genital behavior, frustration and anger result when the implicit promise of genital sex is not kept.

As in previous scenarios, individuals have different intentions here, too. For instance, a man can focus on a woman's body in order to behave genitally. The woman may sense this and stop the transaction, or she may encourage it. Similarly, a person's mode of behavior and dress may be intended to be aesthetically sexual, but be misinterpreted instead as an invitation to pursue more intimacy. It is important to know one's own and the other's intentionality.

Functional, affective sexuality can be illustrated in social behavior that involves qualities such as consideration and warmth. When a man acts as a gentleman and a woman as a lady, they show graceful consideration for others. Demonstrating a sense of humor or kidding another in a light and easy way involves affective sexuality. Some clothing styles may be functionally as well as aesthetically affective.

An example of functional affective sexuality is a hostess at a social gathering. Her behavior is neither explicitly spiritual or aesthetic nor primarily physical. The way she acts is mainly in service of a social and functional situation. She can be graceful and charming, warm and kind, considerate and friendly. Instead of being merely functional, task-oriented, and highly cognitive, she also behaves affectively. She shows she is a person of flesh and blood, not simply a cold function. Unfortunately, however, her affectivity can be misinterpreted as an overture to more intimate relations, since men are prone to assume that affectivity, especially in a social situation, is a come-on.

Similarly, a man can function affectively as a waiter. His sexuality is not directed toward more intimacy nor is it spiritual or aesthetic. Although his service may be an art, it is also a function. He shows a sophisticated style, is socially gracious, and perhaps entertaining. Without affective sexuality, he can easily behave as a robot—a cold rather than a warmly functional person.

Ideally, outside of a marital context, affective sexuality should be an end in itself and not a means to genital gratification. Within marriage, affective sex can engender healthy genital relations as well as its being an end in itself. In short, lay single, vowed celibate, and married people (except with their spouse) can practice all forms of sexuality except genital behavior.

HETEROSEXUAL INTIMACY

To further understand affective sexuality, let us reflect on a man who acts differently in the company of a woman and how he can learn from her in ways that he cannot or seldom learns from a man. Likewise, a woman feels and behaves differently when she is with a man than when she is with a woman. In this sense, men without women and women without men fail to become whole persons. Let us explore some problems, challenges, and opportunities of heterosexual intimacy.

Think of a man and woman dining together and having an enjoyable time. If their dining is usually frequent and private, they are likely to move from friendship to more intimacy. Private, and romantic settings, regularly enjoyed, usually promote experiences that engender desires for greater intimacy. Indeed, the man and woman can be honest with themselves and each other and know their boundaries. Otherwise, "love games" under the cloak of friendship may emerge, or greater intimacy is promised but not delivered. Nevertheless, this man and woman can and should express their primary and affective sexuality. If they repress their affection, they will become cold and insipid. They may speak well, but they lack the "touchabiltiy" and spirit of caring persons.

When we promote the erotic and exclude the spiritual component of affective sexuality, we can easily evoke genital desires that lead to either frustration or satisfaction. For example, a party can and should include healthy affective sexuality. A gathering, however, that promotes the physical-erotic and represses the aesthetic and spiritual increases the probability of physical or genital intimacy. In short, intimate physical dancing, erotic flirting, genital talk, touching games, and promotions of erotic fantasy are likely to generate the erotic genital rather than the erotic-aesthetic—or, a more integrated sexual presence.

Whether we are unmarried people (single or vowed celibate) or married, we need to love others and be committed to healthy and holy living. Imagine a religious brother and sister whose friendship occasionally moves toward erotic intimacy. They express their love in a loving glance or in a chaste touch, but they are careful that their affection is interwoven with aesthetic and spiritual qualities. Facing each other as whole persons, their erotic feelings are less likely to promote genital feelings. If they do become genitally aroused, they can remain within their celibate boundaries. They neither repress nor satisfy erotic and genital desires; rather, they affirm their desires and freely choose not to act on them. At times they may be frustrated and dislike their "no" (to genital gratification), but they freely, though perhaps reluctantly, put limits on themselves. Their "no" is based on a more fundamental "yes"—a yes to their values, love, and primary commitment. This same resolve can characterize the sexual choices of single and married persons.

Indeed, it is possible to hold false notions of chastity and celibacy that impede intimacy. Chastity does not mean sexlessness; it is an experience of integrated (whole) and chaste (pure) loving sex. Chaste persons see and relate to others and self as whole beings, not as fragmented persons. By isolating their physical, functional, or spiritual dimensions from one another, individuals become less than they are. They become "impure"—not purely whole.

Heterosexual intimacy can be especially problematic for people who have repressed their sexuality. Consider a man who represses his sexuality and enters a heterosexual relationship. Though he cares deeply, he is torn with conflict: His repressed sexual needs strongly seek satisfaction, while his standards prevent awareness of his desires. If gratification occurs, he is likely to feel guilty and perhaps ashamed. Or, on the contrary, he could feel a sense of license in seeking genital gratification.

Another example is a woman sexually fixated in early adolescence. Although she is mature in most areas, sexually she is a young adolescent because she never had much opportunity to explore, understand, and integrate sex. If she becomes involved with a man, she may experience sexual desires that her adolescent attitudes fail to integrate. She may act as an adolescent or become too dependent on the man, minimizing her autonomy. Or being naïve, she may be a prime candidate for exploitation. Whatever happens, her challenge is to work through her sexual fixation before she makes important decisions regarding sexual intimacy.

When we attempt to work through sexual repression or fixation, sexual desires may surface too quickly and intensely, and a common consequence is to feel guilty because our standards are incongruent with our experiences. We experience the conflict of intensely feeling one way and just as intensely thinking the opposite. Again, the challenge is to listen to both our thoughts and feelings and to come to a healthier resolution.

Conversely, some people say that they are guiltless. They reason that "if it feels right, it is right." Although feelings seldom lie, their truth is not always the best truth. The popular ethic: "If it feels right, go for it," can be dangerous and destructive to self and others. Such an ethical principle can justify almost any well-intentioned but wrong sexual act.

Some say that if you are sincere and honest, then your behavior is good. Although honesty and sincerity are ways to truth, the "honesty and sincerity" ethic can serve self-gratification instead of the truth of love. For instance, an individual can consciously be sincere and honest but unconsciously use another. One can hide selfish intentions behind a façade of honesty and rationalize questionable behavior with a plea of sincerity. Such an individual can sincerely and honestly violate love. Simply stated, mad or bad behavior can be sincere and honest.

Another challenge of heterosexual intimacy occurs when married people are friends of the opposite sex. Unlike celibates, married persons commit themselves to each other. When a spouse regularly spends private time in a relationship outside marriage, the relationship can gradually edge toward a greater intimacy as well as take time and energy away from his or her marriage.

Consider the man who informs his wife that he is going to dine with a new female employee. He may tell his wife that the woman is lonely and needs help to adjust to her new job and living situation. He sincerely feels obliged to help her. His wife, though hesitant and ambivalent, initially accepts this situation. But if the man calls his wife a few nights later explaining that the new employee still requires his support, his wife may feel more uncomfortable. She knows intuitively that such situations nurture deeper intimacy as well as taking away time and space from his spousal intimacy. This does not mean that married people cannot have friends besides their spouse. Indeed, married persons can and should have friendships that are based on primary and affective sexuality. To understand this better, let us look at friendship in relation to sexuality.

FRIENDSHIP

Virtually everyone wants to have and to be a friend. Some people seek friends to escape loneliness and boredom; some measure their personal success by the number of their friends—they feel guilty or ashamed if they have no friends; others, more cautious, withdraw from potential friendships because of fear or uncertainty. Some people believe that friendship is necessary to live a significantly meaningful life; others are open to friendship but feel content without intimate ones. Finally, there are people who maintain and nourish their friendships throughout their lives.

Friendship comes in various degrees and kinds. Some friends grow closer throughout their life time, while others are friends at certain times in their lives. Some friends like to be with each other in any situation. Others enjoy each other, primarily at work or at social gatherings, and some genuinely play together but not suffer together. The friendship where two persons can share everything with trust, dependability, respect, and fidelity is relatively rare. Such a friendship can evoke the most painful problems, and yet it can have the greatest rewards. Having three or four of these relationships is improbable. One is enough.

The love that characterizes friendship involves standing by, counting on, supporting, and defending each other not only in the relatively easy and enjoyable times but also in the more difficult and risky times. Friends muster the courage to be available to each other no matter what. Like other forms of love, authentic friendship is an end in itself; it needs no justification. Friends do not look for special gains or rewards; neither do they seek approval or a safe way of being liked or affirmed. True friendship is not parasitic. Rather, it strives towards unconditional and respectful concern for the other. Friendship is chaste love.

Unchaste friendship involves manipulation or exploitation. For example, a dependent man may satisfy a "friend's" need to dominate as well as his own need to be dependent. Such a relationship is unchaste because it is based on mutual need satisfaction rather than on giving to and supporting each other's welfare. Instead of promoting healthy growth, these individuals become fixated in a submissive-domineering relationship. Although such a relationship may seem chaste in contrast to overt sexual exploitation, it is nevertheless unchaste. Our challenge is to "purify" ourselves—to uncover and control our hidden unchaste motives.

In the best friendships, whether heterosocial or homosocial, friends ought to express their primary and affective sexuality. An affirmative statement, a nourishing support, a warm glance, and assuring touch, and a respectful embrace can demonstrate concern for the other. Genital relations can also be a meaningful and enjoyable expression of their love, but intuition (as well as clinical and empirical evidence) tells us that genital sex would change their friendship and potentially destroy it. Although some friends may sometimes yearn for genital relations, they can freely choose, albeit with reluctance, to say no to genital encounter in service of a yes to their love.

In a certain sense, every deep and authentic friendship is particular. Friends see each other unlike anyone else sees them; they have and are something special. Such intimate friendships are especially available and fruitful for celibates. Being free from the marital commitment to another human being can allow celibates to be free for intimate friendships. Although married people may have intimate friendships outside marriage, there is the caveat that such friendships, especially heterosexual ones, can hinder the growth of their marital relationship. Perhaps married persons should foster their particular and exclusive friendship within the marriage In a sense, a married person's best friend should be his or her spouse.

ROMANTIC LOVE

Romantic love is in many ways the most affective form of love. It is the love of romantic writers, of youth, of those falling in love. It is the love that activates all our senses; it is never dull and mundane.

What happens when you fall romantically in love? Initially you feel as though you are walking on clouds and that everything is possible. You experience the other as perfect; imperfections are secondary at best. Feeling intensely and often erotically attracted, you feel smitten and strongly involved with the ideal. You idealize each other, feeling you can do and share anything and be your most perfect selves. You feel what love can be without its limits—and, you want to give, to be, and to receive all that is possible. You may feel you want to live together forever, to capture this love forever. Romantic love is one of the most exciting, pleasurable, satisfying, energizing, and seductive experiences. There is a special magic; romantic love can be so intense and total that sometimes it seems like a fantasy that will disappear at any moment.

Romantic lovers experience new possibilities, test their limits, risk their vulnerability, feel more alive than ever before, and they are willing to do almost anything. They may feel that everything is possible and all right, and that life is rich and full. Romantic relationships usually inspire us to become our best selves; new energy and courage provide the way.

Romantic experiences are possible even in solitude. For instance, you may intensely feel the spiritual possibilities of contemplation. Or you may discover a world of meaning that is transcendent and permanent. Asking ultimate questions and being confronted with mysterious issues can engender a peak experience. The joy of contemplation enables you to experience life infinitely. Everything takes on a new meaning.

Romantic lovers—vowed celibate, single, or married—initially experience the unlimited potential of each other and celebrate each other's perfection. However, paradise does not last; romantic times are usually followed by jarring revelations of imperfections, and sometimes by withdrawal from each other. Before they know it, romantic lovers may find themselves criticizing and obsessing about each other's imperfections.

It is not uncommon for a couple in love to begin doubting their love after their honeymoon period. Having once divinized each other, they now demonize each other. Minor habits may become irritating: one squeezes the toothpaste from the middle, the other from the end. His bathroom habits upset her; her cosmetic behavior annoys him. More seriously, she becomes frustrated and angry because he no longer shows his feelings as he once did. He becomes confused and angry with her constant complaining about his unavailability. Whatever the focus of criticism, they concentrate on each other's dark limits instead of bright possibilities.

It feels like heaven has been replaced with hell.

Another example is a person who experiences a new way of living or a profession as a nearly perfect way of living. For example, particularly in early formation when there is considerable personal affirmation, exploration, and direction, religious life offers extraordinary opportunities for individual and communal growth. However, "re-entry problems" may be experienced when a new religious moves from the novitiate to living in an ordinary community. Community living seems much different than it was in the novitiate or as it was idealized in vocation literature. Discovering inevitable imperfections will feel more like a burden than a joy. Here again, a danger is to identify religious or any life form with its limits and obstacles to growth. There are both problems and opportunities in any personal and professional life.

Imagine two persons who care for each other and become close friends. At first, they may idealize their relationship so that it becomes exclusive. They wonder how they ever lived without each other. If one or both persons have been inhibited in expressing affection, they will feel free now to express themselves without restraint. They feel liberated and more wholly alive. However, this "particular" friendship soon encounters limits and obstacles. For instance, the friends discover they can irritate and confuse each other; they can become hurt, angry, and disappointed. Instead of withdrawing from the situation, both persons can step back and listen to themselves and each other, then hopefully return to renew and deepen their friendship so to include both their positive and negative dimensions.

The challenging ideal is that both light and dark sides of life be integrated; neither should be absolutized. In fact, these experiences point to and affirm what life is: both divine and demonic, light and dark, creative and destructive. When we experience a person as perfect, we can remind ourselves that every person is imperfect. When we have disagreements, we can recall past agreements and agree to disagree. We are challenged to see potential virtue where there is vice, strength where there is weakness, joy where there is sadness, love where there is hate, life where there is death. Courage and vision are needed to move with and grow from life's paradoxical rhythm.

Affective sex is clearly a part of romantic love that is—and should be—particularly enjoyable. But the desire to give one's self totally to another person can present difficulties. The affective and ideal qualities of romantic love drive us toward transcending all and any limits; consequently, we yearn to give ourselves unconditionally in every way possible. Although we may desire to celebrate our love in genital experiences, we can say "no" in service of a "yes" to our love.

Ideally, a radical decision should not be made in either the so-called divine or demonic phases of love. When we are madly in love and experience no imperfections whatsoever—the divine phase, a life commitment is precarious. We should be just as prudent about making radical decisions while in a demonic phase; when life is overwhelmingly dark, any light or relief is tempting. It is better to wait until we make more sense of our life and are freer to choose. For example, a jilted or betrayed person can quickly become emotionally involved on the "rebound" and be especially vulnerable to an understanding and affectionate person. This individual can make decisions he or she will later regret.

A life decision requires that we be open to the limitations set by both the positive and negative factors of individuals and of our past, present, and future situations. For instance, a man who falls in love with a woman may be in the divinizing stage of romantic love. When asked what is wrong with his beloved, he may offer nothing concrete. Until he can clearly state what is positive and negative about her and himself, it is better that he wait before making such a radical decision to get married or remain single.

Conversely, it is tempting to separate when nothing seems right or possible. Experiencing enormous stress, we can be duped into feeling that a change in life-style will solve personal problems. More likely, we will take our problems with us. It is wiser to look at and deal with the dark side in and between ourselves before making decisions.

Authentic committed love is never perfect or divine, but neither is it completely imperfect or demonic. It is a combination of both. If authentic love were perfect, commitment would not be necessary. Love exists for imperfect people struggling to perfect themselves. Because we are a unity of perfection and imperfection, commitment is called for.

Romantic love is important, however, because it can be a prelude to a more committed love. Its power of attraction, gentle excitement, and erotic idealism make it easier, more enjoyable, and exciting for us to enter love. Since love, especially intimate love, is a risky venture, romantic love makes the entry into love relatively easier, safer, and more fun. Without romantic love, some people would never take the risk to love. Romantic love is an intense promise of a more permanent love that is both ideal and limited, erotic and transcendent, for the moment and forever, pleasurable and painful, divine, and demonic—in short, a love that embraces and dignifies all of us.

This does not mean that romantic love is only a means toward an end. When immersed in romantic love, it is good to celebrate and proclaim it. Our experience can be a witness to love that promotes happiness for others. Moreover, it offers a precious source of memories that can help us gain perspective when going through difficult times.

AN AFFECTIONATE DISPOSITION

An affectionate disposition refers to a readiness to love everyone and anyone, anywhere, at any time, as much as possible. Although we cannot be open to everyone at the same time, we can express love to people we see everyday, once a year, or less. Such a loving orientation is normally expressed in the day-to-day activities of work, play, impromptu meetings, and social gatherings. Thoughtfulness, respect, courtesy, compromise, concern, warmth, understanding, sympathy, and compassion can be manifestations of an everyday disposition of affection.

The disposition to love is a key dynamic in good and healthy living. When the opportunity arises, those having this disposition are ready to express affection in the best possible way. They are willing to promote another's welfare as best they can by being friendly, doing a favor, or even withdrawing. Paradoxically, to withdraw from another can sometimes be the best way to love that person. If saying something does more harm than good, perhaps staying out of a person's way is the best form of intimacy. Sometimes giving nothing more than a friendly smile or to be detached from another's problems can be the best form of love.

When everyday affection becomes more intense and intimate, we should try to take responsibility for it. It is unfair to share deeply and then suddenly leave or withdraw, for such intimacy can imply that more love is to come. When unfulfilled promises are not met, pain and often resentment occur. For example, Jane may be sincerely concerned about Joan who is lonely. She listens to Joan's frustrations and helps her realize herself in intimacy. But when Joan grows and seeks a friendship based more on a two-way rather than a one-way relationship, Jane withdraws. For sure, everyday affection can lead to more intimate love such as friendship. When it does, we should be willing and able to take the time and effort to respond justly and honestly rather than making implicit promises we do not intend to or cannot fulfill.

It is usually better to know one another well before we become more intimate; otherwise, such intimacy can be intrusive or chauvinistic. For instance, after knowing a man for an hour, a woman may try to encounter him spiritually. If the man does not intend this kind of direct care as he might in a counseling situation or with a friend, he could feel violated. On the other hand, we can sometimes find ourselves immediately at home with each other and feel safe enough to move closer without conventional preliminaries. To avoid unnecessary pain and to promote healthy relationships, let us reflect on chastity.

CHASTITY

Unfortunately, chastity is often interpreted as an impediment to or repression of sexuality. In fact, chastity promotes and nourishes healthy behavior, for it combats our tendencies to be selfish, exploitative, and manipulative.

Chastity is respectful and unconditional concern. As chaste persons, we act with respect: we take a second look at reality and seek its deeper meaning. Rather than experiencing one another only as physical or functional beings, we strive to see, appreciate, and respond to our whole personhood. To see people as disembodied—only as spiritual, can also be unchaste. To repress one's sexuality, for example, can be an unchaste act. To separate one's sexuality from spirituality, or spirituality from sexuality, is unchaste. Chastity means to experience and to respect another as a whole person. Chastity is the virtue by which sexuality and spirituality are dynamically interrelated.

Chaste people try to promote what is good. Not acting simply to satisfy their own needs, they strive to do what is best for self and other—for the growth of community. Chastity involves behaving with unconditional care, without the impurities of exploitation and manipulation. Chaste persons try to purge themselves of hidden agendas. Chaste behavior is pure.

Chastity demands that we transcend such impurities as lust, manipulation, exploitation, domination, arrogance, narcissism, selfishness, pride, dependency, and neediness. Acting only out of physical desires alone is unchaste because it involves treating self and others only as physical beings. Manipulation for self-satisfaction is also unchaste because it lacks concern and respect. Exploitation and patronizing on any sexual level—primary, genital, or affective—is unchaste. For example, a man may be unchaste when he oppresses, pulls rank, or withdraws from a woman; a woman may be unchaste when she is masochistic, obsequious, or hostile. Rather than manipulating or using one another, we can take care to respond integrally.

Chastity also can help us to purge negative defense mechanisms. For instance, we are not chaste simply because we abstain from genital gratification. To undervalue ourselves as men or women, to rigidly control affective sexuality, and to repress genital sexuality are modes of unchaste behavior. In a sense, sexless people are unchaste.

Passive dependence can also be a violation of chastity. For instance, when a man inordinately depends on others for affection, or tries to please and serve them to manipulate them to satisfy his own needs, he is unchaste. It is unchaste to suck the life out of people, to do anything as long as one is accepted and cared for. A woman who invites a man to dominate or manipulate her is unchaste. A woman who encourages a man to exploit her genitally (even within marriage) is unchaste. To be sure, the man is also unchaste.

Chastity requires discipline to control one's life—to practice ways that promote free expression of truth. Chaste persons are dedicated to awareness of and control of the impurities that prevent them from being their best selves. They are careful of overestimating or underestimating the value of self and others. Interpersonally, they break through normal facades and games to be more available to others. Their freedom from the pollution of bias, egoism, and neediness frees them for healthy love.

Unchaste sexual behavior means that the centripetal (ingoing) force of mere sex, especially genital sex, impedes or destroys the centrifugal (outgoing) movement of unconditional love. Loveless sex is a violation of chastity because it works against healthy interpersonal relations. Sex without care, however, is not the only violation of chastity. The will-to-power, as evidenced in exploitation, can be just as harmful as loveless and perfunctory sex. Even though chastity is necessary for healthy and holy living, some people consider vowed chastity and celibacy to be senseless. One reason religious vow chastity is to underline the importance and significance of chastity for everyone.

Nevertheless, vowed celibates can be unchaste in subtle ways as well as explicit ones. For example, the priest who only counsels lonely, frustrated, and attractive women may be unchaste; his concern for a woman's welfare may in fact conceal an attempt to satisfy his own needs. To probe her inner life, especially her sexual life, can satisfy his own needs while giving him a sense of being "holy." It is not holy, however; such countertransference is unchaste because it primarily serves one self and not others.

Perhaps as many offenses against chastity are committed within marriage as outside of it. For instance, sexual intercourse without love is unchaste. To defend herself and protest against such sexual barbarism, a woman may become sexually dysfunctional—perhaps the only way she can say no to a man's unchaste behavior. A man is also unchaste when he pulls rank on his wife or takes her for granted. Some men have been programmed to place women in roles that are in service of men. Their sexist expectations are unchaste.

A married woman's unchaste behavior may be more subtle. Perhaps she treats her husband like a son or another child. If she is flirtatious, yet consistently withdraws from more intimacy, she can be unchaste. She may use genital sexuality to manipulate her husband: instead of confronting him with the real issues, she punishes him by refusing genital relations. Moreover she may say, "if you do what I say, then I will satisfy you." If he accedes, both partners of the contract are unchaste.

In many ways, lay celibates may have the most difficult time practicing chastity. Unlike married or religious persons, single persons usually do not have the support and affirmation of a community. In the throes of loneliness, single persons may feel pressure to seek sexual fulfillment without committed love. In the next chapter, we will see that although sex without love can be a pleasurable and satisfying experience, the fulfillment is temporary and it fails to promote wholistic growth.

Single women are particularly susceptible to unchaste treatment. Too many men are willing to take advantage of a woman's loneliness and offer her caricatures of care. Of course, women can encourage such exploitation or actively exploit. Recreational sex may seem better than nothing. Although unchaste behavior may be normal, human, and meaningful, it is neither healthy nor good.

In short, chastity is a virtue that promotes a good and healthy life. Chaste people, married or unmarried, are respectful and loving. They abstain from exploitative, manipulative, and deceptive behavior. They do not regard sex as something to use or simply a source of pleasure. Rather, they see and celebrate in chastity the mystery—the spirit—of sex.

Chapter Five
Genital Sexuality

Standards for acceptable sexual behavior have changed considerably in the past forty years. Not long ago, many people followed a code of sexual restriction and repression; today, freedom without much constraint is more normative. Both of these extremes—the new sexual license and the old sexual bondage—are less than healthy. We now turn to consider immature and unhealthy as well as healthy ways of dealing with genital desires. The consequences of positive and negative approaches, the appeal and effects of experiences such as masturbation, pornography, and intercourse, and how genital feelings can promote wholistic growth are discussed. Before presenting these specific topics, however, let us consider some normative structures and dynamics of genital sexuality.

HEALTHY GENITAL SEX

A common mistake is to identify sexuality with genitality, understandably so, because books, articles, and lectures about sex are usually about genital sex. As we have seen, sexuality can also be understood in its primary and affective forms. Although genital sex is one of three types, it has been overemphasized at the expense of the others. However, genital sex is essential to humankind—and, it offers special problems and possibilities.

Genital sexuality is defined as behavior, thoughts, fantasies, and desires that activate the genital organs. It is important to make the distinction between genital feelings of genitality and genital behavior. Genital intercourse and masturbation, for example, are explicit forms of genital behavior. Desires and fantasies that may or may not lead to such genital gratification are modes of genitality. Everyone, more or less, has genital feelings, and is therefore genital; however, these feelings can be or need not be acted upon. In short, feelings are neutral, but what we do with them determines the presence or absence of health.

Genital sexuality is an essential part of ourselves, but when we identify the human person with genital sex alone, we treat others and ourselves as less than we really are. Genital sex is one important expression, not the totality of primary sex, of being a man and a woman.

When we misuse or abuse genital sexuality, we violate ourselves. To use someone's genitals merely for gratification is to mistreat that person, or it is as if he or she is only "a body"—"some-body." But when we actualize our genitality in healthy ways, we celebrate and actualize ourselves. Healthy genital sex involves caring for the whole person—body, mind, and spirit—and not just "a body."

Central to this analysis is the understanding that genital sexuality contains a dynamic force that urges us to go beyond self to others. This "transcendent movement" in genital sex (as in all forms of sex) points to its relational quality. Genitality seeks more than self, extending toward another, urging us to seek union with another.

Think of how our genital organs change when we are sexually aroused. We move toward each other to give and receive. The penis and clitoris as well as other sex organs seek contact, connection, and union beyond themselves. Arousal can be mainly physical, but just as often or moreso it is cognitive, affective, and spiritual. Genital changes are visible confirmations of our desire to be "in union with."

Sexuality is a sign that we are more than individuals, that we tend toward community. This unitive, transcendent movement can be considered the spiritual dimension of sexuality. Moreover, genital sexuality is one of the clearer signs of spirituality—of our call to love. In genital intercourse, two people move toward each other and to receive each other. The spirit of genital sex powerfully urges a person to be one with another, to give oneself and consequently to be more fully oneself.

Along with seeking union or love, genital sex also fosters life. The possibility of procreation bears witness to the transcendence or sacredness of genital sex. The possibility of conception affirms that in genital sex we go beyond our individual selves, and the inability to procreate implies the normative ability. Any attempt to control this potential affirms its existence.

Genitality clearly manifests the transcendent dynamic or spiritual quality of sexuality. To nourish this thirst to go beyond ourselves to foster community, a genuine commitment of love is necessary. Only love (spirit) is sufficient to meet this spiritual demand of genital sex. Only steadfast love can keep the transcendence of genitality in harmony with healthy growth. Mere physical and psychosocial satisfactions are inappropriate and inadequate responses to the spiritual call of genital sex. Without the spiritual dimension, genital sex eventually dissipates into anxious emptiness. Indeed, genital behavior can be fun and meaningful without love, but it is less than healthy. It starves the spirit as one futilely tries to nourish oneself with satisfaction and success. Being less than whole (and therefore less than healthy), the individual ends up being isolated rather than in communion.

Along with transcendence, sex involves embodiment, and therefore it necessarily involves time and space. Too often we minimize the importance of the obvious: since we are embodied or situated spirits, healthy genital sex requires a proper time and space. When people do not have or take the proper time, their experience is usually impeded and eventually causes distress.

For example, a married couple chooses to enjoy sex before their busy routines begin. However, if they frequently rush their genital gratification, they will create an experience far from what it could and should be. Interestingly, the sexes usually have different needs in this regard. Women, for instance, would be especially sensitive to rushed and careless sex. Men, however, though not all, can engage more easily in "hurried sex."

A woman's primary sexuality inclines her to integrate genital experience with other experiences such as love and affection, and this process usually takes more time. A man, however, is more prone to separate his experiences or to focus exclusively on genital sex, which takes less time. For instance, when a man pressures a woman to "hurry," she will usually feel tense or turned off.

If genital sexuality is performed quickly, it soon loses its vitality and spirit. For sure, mere satisfaction can occur quickly, but an encounter between persons usually takes time. Making love involves more than having sex. Embodiment means that time is important in giving oneself to another.

Here are one woman's comments on hurried sex. "What really turns me off is when my boyfriend insists on having sex. It seems so urgent to him, like nothing else matters—including me. It's like the most important thing is to have an orgasm, the sooner the better. Then everything's all right. Not for me. Sometimes it's exciting, but mainly it leaves me empty and frustrated. Mere sex simply doesn't fulfill me and, besides, it leaves me wanting."

Not only sufficient time but also the right space is needed to foster and enjoy the sacred dimension of genital sex. "Car sex" may be fun initially, but it soon becomes physically and psychologically cramped. An apartment or a pleasure resort, although affording more comfort, is usually tentative, temporary, and perhaps precarious. The lack of a place where a couple can feel securely at home will eventually evoke tension that impedes healthy sexuality.

Without consistent and proper time and space, genital behavior is at best less than it can be, and if nothing else, it becomes unwieldy. When couples find themselves planning genital relations, regulating the time, or hurrying the experience, they soon become tense and frustrated. Being discreet, moving from place to place, or planning meetings become tiring and contrived. Scheduling sex works against the rhythm and nurturance of healthy sex. Secure, comfortable time and space are needed for two persons (body, mind, and spirit) to encounter each other. Healthy sex calls for love and affection; these take more time and better space than physical sex affords. Less than healthy sex becomes disassociated from the rest of life instead of becoming an integral and healthy part of life.

Only a marital situation can offer the proper time and place for healthy sexual relations. Premarital and extramarital sex can be meaningful and pleasurable, but the scheduling of time and finding a space engenders distress that impedes on-going growth. Even if there is love, such genital expression will, in the long run, hinder the growth of love. Yes, nonmarital sex can be an expression and affirmation of love, but the situation threatens the free progress of love; it can even destroy it. On the other hand, marriage does not always provide appropriate time and place either, nor does it guarantee healthy sex. Nevertheless, marriage—unlike nonmarital life styles—is the only situation wherein the proper time and place (on a long-term basis) are available to foster healthy and loving genital relations.

As noted earlier, genital sex is not only a pleasurable encounter but is also a sacred mode of communication. In sex, we go beyond ourselves and out to another. In genital relations we are called to be responsible to each other not only for the moment but also for a life time. Genital sex calls for a lifetime commitment of fidelity and love. The intimacy of genital sex is so imminent and transcendent that it can only be nurtured with the imminence and transcendence of love.

The normative principle is this: When we lack a permanent commitment of fidelity and love as well as time and space that marriage offers, genital relations fail to promote healthy (wholistic) growth. Though nonmarital sex may be meaningful and satisfying, it does not engender on-going, wholistic growth. The necessary components for healthy sex are proper time, appropriate place, and authentic commitment. These can be found only in marriage.

However, living life is not as simple as theorizing about life. It can be difficult to abstain from genital sex, especially when in the throes of love. Knowing that sex outside of marriage will not foster healthy growth may seem like a weak and abstract reason when faced with the immediate rewards of genital expression. Having considered the normative principles, let us consider the clinical and pastoral sense and nonsense of genital behavior.

MOTIVATIONS FOR GENITAL GRATIFICATION

Motivations describe the "why," "how," and "what for" of behavior. Motivations are biological, psychosocial, and spiritual forces that urge us to act in one way rather than another. Let us consider some reasons, positive and negative, that pressure us to act in one way rather than another.

Satisfaction, Pleasure, and Fun

It may sound trite, but sex is usually fun. A powerful lure of sex is its carefree quality that fosters a kind of playful celebration of life. Not only genital behavior itself but also and perhaps especially coming to genital play can involve much fun. The preludes to sex, its affective expressions, flirting, testing limits, and fore-play can be filled with fun. Even in less than healthy forms of sexual fun, from pornography to sadomasochism, fun can offer relief, particularly to people who rarely have fun. From the isolated non-productive person to the engaged workaholic, sexual fun offers a pleasant relief. When we have little fun, sex beckons us.

Sexual fun can run the gamut from healthy to unhealthy. Sadomasochistic fun, for example, is far from healthy and usually pathological. Listen to Jan. "What can I say? I know that our sex is a bit kinky and out of bounds, but we do have fun. Something about the sight of blood, his and mine, turns me on more than any other kind of sex. I don't know if you would call it fun, but it sure feels like fun. We don't really hurt ourselves, at least seriously, but we do inflict some minor wounds. Without this type of harmless injury, it just doesn't make it. I get the feeling that there might be something sick about this, but nevertheless it's fun. And, what harm is done except to the two of us? Since, we both agree, what's wrong with that?"

More on the healthy side of sexual fun is Janet's description. "Tom and I really have fun when we have sex. We giggle, laugh, play, tickle, stimulate, explore, play games, whatever gives us wholesome fun. One reason we look forward to being together is because we have fun. We turn each other on, tease and tantalite each other. We feel invigorated and very much alive and yet very much together. Although this is not our only sexual dance, it is the most fun."

To use Janet's metaphor of the dance, there are other forms of dances as well. For instance, some sex, while not being fun, is nevertheless enjoyable. Once again listen to Janet. "Not all of our sex is fun, but neither is it the opposite of fun. Some of our sex is more enjoyable than fun. These are the more quiet and tender moments. There are times when nothing is said and yet we listen in silence. Our touch is slower, our gaze is longer, and our hearing is more attentive. We linger and rest rather than frolicking and being rambunctious. It is a slower dance where the rhythm is more of the spirit than of the body. The music is more silent and serene, the beat is slower and deeper, and the message more transcendent and lasting."

Closely related to fun is pleasure—a rapid rhythm of tension and relief. Although sex is not necessarily pleasurable, it should, more or less, foster pleasure. Besides reducing tension, increasing comfort, and engendering rest, sex satisfies needs that evoke pleasure. Sex is tantalizing, exciting, and as we have seen, fun and enjoyable. A powerful motive for having sex is that the pleasure of sex often exceeds other forms of pleasure while being in the context of some form of closeness and self-disclosure. Sex can be pleasurable in an interpersonal relationship that is very tactile, close, and immediate.

Sexual pleasure is easy to attain and offers immediate gratification. We need not be disciplined to wait for the reward of sex; we can count on sex being pleasurable. Masturbation is usually available and a prostitute can be purchased; non-marital sex is common; and marital sex is attainable more often than not.

Sometimes, however, we must work at achieving the playful pleasure of sex. We must "come on" to another, try to make the other, give a line, or be patient, thoughtful, kind, and caring. But once we are in the arena of sexuality, the pleasure comes more easily. For most, the effort to achieve sexual pleasure is worth the effort. "Although I don't score every Friday night, when I do, it is worth every dollar and ounce of energy", explains Harry. "Sometimes I don't meet a girl or pick up someone, but when I do, it motivates me to try again. The pleasure far surpasses anything else; so it's well worth the effort and periodic frustration The excitement and satisfaction of exploring new territory are high rewards for such effort."

Sexual pleasure is readily available and comes easy in solitary sex. Masturbation is accessible at almost any time and is easily accomplished. It is practically an absolute guarantee of pleasure. Particularly if one's life is filled with stress and void of pleasure, masturbation can be very attractive. It satisfies needs, reduces tension, and offers pleasure. For instance, the pleasure of masturbation can offer the workaholic or thinkaholic needed balance. To abstain from masturbation leaves many in a state of tension and frustration, and to masturbate offers pleasurable relief and comfort.

From this perspective, it seems foolish to abstain from masturbation.

Think of how sexual satisfaction can be used as a method of stress management. Sex usually lessens stress and can enable us to manage more effectively. Reducing stress and affirming self and other can engender momentary peace. Sex can help us to calm down and be less uptight, to unwind and to settle down. Orgasm is both a metaphor and a reality of ecstatic tranquility. In sex, we can, at least for a few moments, come to rest.

Ecstasy

To be sexual is to be ecstatic. The etymologies of ecstatic (*ec-stasis*, "to stand out") and of sex, (*secare*, "to split or to seek the other half") indicate how ecstasy and sexuality are related. Sexuality moves us beyond ourselves, to seek another, to look at another, to touch another. By its very nature, sex is relational, and the dynamic structure of sex is ecstatic.

"It means a lot to me when my wife is sexually turned on and comes to me," says Brian. "Especially when she takes the initiative, I know she desires me. Being the only one she desires to give herself to, inviting me to come to her is mind blowing. Sure, she turns me on physically, but even moreso, my wife humbles me. Here is this beautiful and precious woman beckoning me to caress her, to make love to her, to be one with her. She presents herself in her naked vulnerability to see and touch her as nobody else. What a gift.

"Really, I'm in a different world. I forget about everything else and can be just with her. I don't want to sound corny, but our love life does make life worth living. Without losing myself in my wife, I'm not sure what I'd do. What a void there would be."

In sex, we literally stand out. The sexual organs of both sexes, more obviously with men, move toward connection. Not only do the genital organs desire union, but the secondary characteristics stand out as well. Such physiological changes are manifestations of the dynamic nature of sexuality. Sex seeks to go beyond itself to be in union with another, and at least temporarily, it gives some peace and comfort. Sexual union is a powerful attraction for anyone and especially for alienated people.

Sex is also ecstatic in a more ordinary sense of getting turned on, tuned in, and high on sex. In a very real sense, we move into a world that differs from our everyday world. In this sense, sex is a pleasant escape from the humdrum, stressful everyday life. In sex, we get away from the ordinary and move toward the extraordinary.

Part of sexual ecstasy often includes a kind of freedom and a relatively safe way of risking oneself. There is freedom of exposing oneself, of letting go, and of testing limits as well as freedom from stress, mundane living, and inhibitions. There is also risk of being vulnerable, hurt, exposed, and shamed. An alluring paradox of sex is that it offers security as well as risk.

Some sex is recreational, for in a sense we re-create ourselves in sexuality. By going beyond ourselves with mutual affirmation and playful fun, we become more than our "static" selves; we become "ec-static." Indeed, although such recreation may not come from the depths of our being, there is some creativity. We can evoke and provoke each other to be more than we ordinarily are. Even crass recreational sex involves some spirit that calls us beyond ourselves.

This woman has a similar yet very different view than Brian had toward ecstasy. "I kid you not. When I see a man's erection, I get turned on. Watching his penis grow, seeing it stand out, and reaching me, wanting to penetrate me makes me come alive. I know he desires me, and is willing to do almost anything to get into me. Ah, what power—in him and moreso in me.

"Even when it's a short term affair, I feel good about his desiring me. And I feel my body move toward him. My body changes and opens up to receive him. It's as if I'm in a different world. It's so different than the drag of work or the boredom of home. In sex, I enter a place where I vibrate with life. Sure, I know there can be dangers, but it's worth the risk. It sure beats boredom or being treated as a nobody."

Sex also affirms our bodies/ourselves. When someone values or simply takes pleasure in our bodies, we know that we are, to some extent, worthwhile. Like the previous woman, even when used, we may rationalize that at least we are worthy of being used, which may feel better than indifference. By drawing us into reality, sex combats avoidance and isolation as well as a detached cerebral style of living. As Jake explains: "I have a high tech computer job that gets me involved in a very cerebral world. In sex it is as if I come back to earth and really feel alive. I get away from the abstract and intellectual world into a concrete physical world. Without sex, I'm afraid that I might drift away into a virtual reality."

One of the paradoxes of sex is that its ecstasy is sensuous and at times voluptuous. The embodied ecstasy of sex is tactile. Even from a distance sex touches us. Skin touches skin; flesh emerges with flesh. For practically anyone, the incarnated transcendence of sex is a powerfully appealing force that pulls us together. The intimate touch of another transforms us, inviting us to come out of our individuality to communion.

In the symphony of sex, all our senses can come together. The sight of sex invariably catches our attention. The sounds of sex have many melodies that resonate within us. Likewise, the smell and taste of sex draw us to the intimate intricacies of aroused bodies. Sex can be a feast of the senses.

Validation

Indeed, the transformative touch of sex is not always in service of reciprocal growth. One's touch can use another for self-gratification. Touch can hinder rather than promote union, harm rather than heal, disrupt rather than comfort, irritate rather than sooth.

Nevertheless, to engage in sex is usually a validating experience in a myriad of ways. As the etymology of validated indicates (*valere* = to be strong), sex can strengthen and empower. In sex, we feel valued—worthy of being desired. Sex gives us a vibrant sense of reality, grounding us in concrete and sensual reality. We are taken out of intellectual and fantasy worlds to affectively real ones. Rather than being isolated, we are in some way worthy of connection. And nothing is more important to mental health than interpersonal contact.

Sex is an intimate "yes" to our being worthwhile. Even in the most recreational sex, we are in some way valued. Loveless sex can give us a fleeting glimpse of what loving sex gives. Loveless sex can, for a time, be an analgesic that numbs our pain and offers illusionary hope. Often, precarious and temporarily validation feels better than the pain of isolation and worthlessness.

The validation of sex motivates us to seek sex, sometime to the extent of addiction. In spite of our intellectual awareness of the limitations of physical sex, we can find ourselves yearning for its validation. We can feel compelled to seek in sex the validation of our body, personality, and soul in spite of knowing that its validation is temporary. We can feel powerless when sex enters us with the illusion of validation and completeness.

Loveless sex or sex with little spirit may feel good for the moment, but its validation quickly dissipates. Thus, abstinence is initially difficult but overall a better way. Abstinence is a "no" to spiritless sex and a "yes" to sex that seeks the more permanent and fulfilling validation. Abstinence says "no" to the illusions of sex and yes to its healthy realities.

"To be honest, my husband treats me like crap. He always has to be right; he treats me with no respect; he wants to be served; he takes me for granted, etc., etc. He's just a big, spoiled selfish kid. I hate him.

"But in sex, he's different. His touch, his presence, his looks are different. He's almost gentle and thoughtful. He almost cherishes me. He certainly wants me, and unlike most of our life, he is willing to give. His touch is magic. For a while, my problems disappear. For a few fleeting moments, I feel worthwhile. Maybe there is hope for our marriage, to my life.

"Sure, I know it's temporary, but it's real too. It's as if I'm usually in a desert and sex is a life-saving oasis. The pain disappears, and I get a feel for what life can be. Even when I know I'm being used, I still feel desired and valued. It feels a lot better than anxious nothingness.

"Now, unfortunately and probably fortunately, sex is wearing thin. I feel more used than valued, and the hope of finding true intimacy is almost dead. This scares me. At least with sex there was some pleasure, some hope, some feeling of worth. Now there is nothing."

This woman shows how sex can offer healing hope. Although sex can engender hope for a better life, the promises of sex dissipate without an overall life of love. The analgesic illusory power of sex eventually wanes, and the pain of a loveless life takes over. Instead of feeling validated and hopeful in sex, she feels used and disillusioned.

Simon tells a similar story. Simon has been married for twenty-three years to a woman who has a borderline personality disorder. At times she can be passionately caring and fun, and suddenly be just as passionately hostile and critical. Other times she can be withdrawn, cold, and indifferent. Negativity permeates her existence, and she can never admit to being wrong. Thus, she will do anything to win, including publicly humiliating

Simon, rejecting him, and simply being mean. Flirting with other men is not rare, and Simon wonders if she has had some affairs.

So, why would Simon remain in such an abusive marriage? Listen to him, "yea, I know, everyone thinks I'm crazy to stay with my wife. But as long as I stay within her narrow framework, I manage to manage. As long as I give her what she wants, don't disagree, and let her be in control, we get along for the most part. Yes, I know I value her more than myself and that I sell myself short. Still, we do have some good times—as long as I....

"It's a bit embarrassing to say, but sex is a big reason I hang in there. And it's not what you might think. Sex is not just a matter of physical gratification; it goes much deeper than that. Sex is the only time when my wife is consistently positive. Unlike the rest of my life with her, in sex she never criticizes, degrades, or shames me. Sex is a different world. For a while, I feel accepted, valued, wanted, and cherished. Rationally, I know that I pay a big price for this validation, but it's all I got."

Indeed, Simon has problems not only with his wife, but also with himself. He is willing to tolerate abuse because of what he receives in sex. In sex, he feels worthwhile, manly, affirmed, and free. Although the rest of his co-dependent life with his wife is like walking through a field of land mines, in sex he feels free and experiences what marriage could be.

Yet, Simon knows that sex is not an adequate answer to the demands of love. Although he experiences some love in sex, its inconsistency coupled with the abuse makes life very difficult. Even loving sex is not a saving grace when it fails to be integrated with more pervasive and reliable love. Indeed, sex lessens pain, gives repose, validates dignity, and offers hope, but without committed love they are temporary and often illusions. Anxiety, desperation, and invalidation are likely to emerge

Without steadfast spirit, sex sooner or later invalidates us. No longer are we seduced by its magical and analgesic power. Rather than being turned on and empowered, we are turned off and weakened. The connection of sex no longer feels intimate but rather an apathetic or even repulsive closeness. Sometimes we can no longer stand the other's touch. Then, the other remains "other," and we are no longer "we."

Spiritless sex engenders shame; it diminishes our worth. Instead of being strengthened, we are weakened. We shrink and want to disappear. Abusive sex—from ordinary loveless sex to rape and incest—invalidates, insults, and violates our worth. Finally, there is often a compelling urge to abstain.

Yet, if sex is the only or primary way we are validated, we may seek that which harms us. If outside of sex, we were never or seldom valued, cherished, desired, or affirmed, we may feel compelled in spite of our best interests to seek sex or to accept loveless sex. To be strong and free, we must have experiences that reliably and validly affirm, strengthen, and liberate our whole beings.

Although we can be healthy without genital sex, we do need the life-giving validation of love. Without love, we cannot be healthy and happy. With, in, and through love, we can learn to abstain from sex or anything that displaces love. When we love ourselves and give and receive love from others, freedom, strength, and serenity reign.

Amelioration

Sexual involvement can include more subtle psychological and spiritual motives. For instance, loneliness can be a powerful motivator. When we feel the presence of the other more in absence, when we yearn to be with another, when we reach out to touch and to be touched, sex can take the sting out of our loneliness. Although love is the only adequate answer to the question of loneliness, sex can initially ameliorate its intensity. In sex, we may experience some care, or at least a pleasant counterfeit. Even in masturbation, we can fill, albeit temporarily, the empty yearning of loneliness. Sex cools the heat, settles the restlessness, and fills the emptiness.

Listen to this celibate priest. "I can't help it that I get horny as hell. And I don't think it's just my testosterone shooting up. I know that this is human, but it's very difficult. Sometimes I am tempted to get involved sexually even though I would violate my vows and probably misuse my power. I truly want to keep the appropriate boundaries. Still, I am left alone with the uncomfortable experience of loneliness. I usually get through it, sometimes by masturbating. I don't like to masturbate because I think it is morally wrong or at least immature. Nevertheless, it does lessen the emptiness and the tension for a while. I know that masturbation is a poor substitute for a real relationship. In fact, it only exacerbates my loneliness."

Although most feelings can urge us to engage in sex, loneliness has a special relationship with sexuality. Loneliness, like sexuality, calls out to the other; they both seek intimacy. Thus, in some respects sexuality is a natural response to loneliness.

Other feelings like boredom, anxiety, and depression can also be motivators for sexual behavior. Sexual satisfaction offers excitement to combat boredom, contentment to extinguish anxiety, fulfillment to ameliorate depression. Sex makes a tantalizing offer: It both excites and tranquilizes, activates and slows down, intensifies and calms. What else can offer this?

In some respects and uniquely so, sex is both an upper and downer. Sex induces excitement, tension, and pleasure and then reduces these feelings, ending in calm and rest. So if our sexual intensity is not resolved, we are left being restless, incomplete, and frustrated. It is like a conductor who stops the orchestra in the middle of a passionate symphony.

A seductive feature of sex is to cause us to forget or escape the tensions of everyday living. It can move us out of our tense everyday world and into an erotic and comfortable world. Faithful lovers, rather than escaping from self, move out of the ordinary world to express and foster their love, so to cope better with everyday living. Certainly, pleasure, comfort, escape, and fulfillment can be consequences of healthy marital sex. To ameliorate tension through marital sex can be a healthy way to receive comfort, to be energized, and to gain perspective on one's primary reason for being: love.

Yearning To Be Whole

Genital sex can generate feelings of being whole. "Wholeness" can especially attract those living fragmented or less than integral lives. For instance, to people who live a "heady" existence, a life "from the neck up," sex can be a way of affirming the rest of the self—especially "from the neck down." A "thinkaholic" – someone who operates from the neck up and only sees truth coming from rational thought – may engage periodically in sex as an attempt to become whole and embodied.

Another expression of the longing for wholeness is striving for self-completion. A man and a woman can complement each other in sexual relations. A man finding "his other half" in a woman and she in him. Genital desires give one of the clearest manifestations of the Yin and Yang seeking completion in each other. Through committed love, a couple becomes one with each other and, paradoxically, each becomes more of himself or herself. By giving, surrendering, and ultimately becoming powerless, one receives the gift of becoming more complete and powerful.

However, if one uses another to affirm one's shaky sense of sexual identity, then sex can be unhealthy or at least immature. This form of "sexploitation" may give the illusion of being what the individual is not—a mature person. Consider the example of a man who brags about being a "man" because of his sexual experiences. It is questionable that he is much of a man. Actually, he is more likely a "playboy"—a little, insecure person who likes to play. Like a child who plays with toys, he plays with people in a sad attempt to convince himself and others that he is a man. Instead of finding one's identity through mere genital sex, such experiences hinder the process.

Without intimacy, we are incomplete, restlessly seeking to be close to another. Sex offers intimacy—close connection. If the powerful attraction of sex is the promise of interpersonal fulfillment and completion, why not indulge in sex? We have indicated that sex with little spirit is a false promise, for its effects are temporary and often leave us emptier and more lonely. It gives us a taste of what can be and then takes it away. It is a humbling illusion. Conversely, sex with spirit (committed love) and in a healthy context engenders and sustains on-going intimacy. Its consequences lessen and comfort our feelings of incompleteness.

In the repose of sex we can experience being whole. It is as if we are one with ourselves and at times with another. We feel completed. We have nothing else to give. We have spent ourselves. Although such an experience of ecstatic wholeness may be fleeting, it pressures us to seek it more extensively and consistently. In sexuality, particularly in orgasm, we are given a powerful hint of what is meant by being whole.

Try to resonate with this sixty-eight year old widow. "It hasn't been easy since my husband suddenly died three years ago. I miss him so much. I miss just being with him—the fun we had together and the intimacy and sex we enjoyed. I remember them with a joyful ache.

"Masturbation doesn't do it. It gives me a frustrating hint of what we had. When I fantasize about George and me, I feel some muted joy and the stimulation excites me. Perhaps it reminds me that I'm still a sexual woman. But it's a poor substitute for what we had.

"With masturbation, it's as if I experience a momentary illusion of the completeness and union I once had. But after orgasm, I feel incomplete and wanting. I feel lonely aloneness just as much or even more. Here I am yearning to give and receive, but no one is there for me. Masturbation only seems to affirm that I am alone.

"Maybe an affair would work, but I doubt it. An affair, it seems to me, is too much like masturbation. Maybe marriage? That's easier said than done, considering how few single men around my age are available. Besides, I really don't want to go through the tedious process of dating. So what am I to do? Abstinence is not easy or pleasant."

Genital sex is special, and it can make us feel special. The unity of transcendent love and sensual pleasure, the ecstatic escape and intimate union, the naked I and thou, the creative power and helplessness, the comforting security and vulnerability, the invigorating fun and rest—are some of the many paradoxes. Genital sexuality's sacred sensuality calls for a privacy that proclaims a public love. Healthy, loving sex is very special. It ought to be celebrated, for it is a sacred (*kairos*) time.

Power

Genital sex can create, co-create, procreate, re-create, transcend, pleasure, control, hurt, violate, sadden, comfort, heal, humor, and unite. It can give and receive, evoke vulnerability and helplessness, provide the security to share oneself, and show or give hints of our best self. Indeed, other forms of intimacy can be just as or more powerful than genital sex. Nevertheless, genital sex has much to offer.

Its power can be less than healthy. For example, manipulation involves handling people as if they were objects to be controlled for one's benefit rather than persons to be respected. Likewise, exploitation involves using others for personal gain. Seducing another with dress and words, taking advantage of an innocent person, or making false promises are power plays intended to manipulate and exploit.

Sex can be used to control and conquer, especially when one feels inferior. The man who feels inferior to or threatened by women may use sex to put women "down" and to give himself the feeling of being "up." A woman mistreated by men may use sex to get even with them. She might, for example, excite men and then withdraw or ridicule them. Such counter phobic behavior is unhealthy.

Hostility under the guise of love can be a powerful motive for genital relations. Some men treat women as inferior or as objects to use for their own satisfaction. They regard women as the enemy—someone to use, lower, or hurt. Men, who harbor hidden fear and resentment are disposed to keep women "lower" and "down" as a way of dealing with their own insecurity. Acting out of hostility is never good or healthy.

The comments of this man betray such an inclination. "Yea, I scored last week. You know, girls are made for men. They're like buses: you get on and get off. There's nothing like balling a broad. What else are women good for? Yea. And there are plenty around who want to play." Underlying this man's crude language, which more aptly describes an athletic contest than love, is inferiority and hostility. He certainly is not the man he pretends to be.

Sex also incorporates the power to co-create, to stand out, to touch, to be with, to excite, to elicit orgasm. In the appropriate context, all of these powers can be healthy. Sex can be a vehicle to manipulate, to exploit, to hurt, to degrade, and to violate. To dominant, to be on top of, to abuse, to ridicule, to reject are all unhealthy forms of power. The power of sex, healthy or unhealthy, can make sex very attractive.

Try to understand this woman. "Why do I have sex with male pigs? Let me tell you. I look at how men, not all mind you, treat women at work. So many are pathetic. They look at you like you're a sex toy. I hate to play the sexism card, but we woman are not treated fairly and are held back, or we have to play sexual games to advance.

"So why do I get sexually involved with these dumb schmucks? Sure, I more or less like being wined and dined, and it probably helps my career. At least, I think it does. More important and subtle is the power I get from sex.

"Sex is where I am in control. Unfaithful bastards become helpless in my arms. I can make them jump through hoops, risk their marriage, and fool them into thinking that I really care. Like a skilled prostitute, I guess. I tell them what they want to hear. I give them the illusion of being a great lover. The pathetic slobs; they don't even know the truth. I don't get high from the sex; sex is a means to an end. The power gets me high."

This woman is angry and probably for some valid reasons. Her resentment motivates her to have sex with men she despises. Sex is her way of being in control of powerful men. For her sex not only evens the score, but also puts her ahead. Paradoxically, her promiscuous sex is a way of trying to keep her dignity.

Indeed, the power of sex can be healthy. We have seen how its power to co-create and procreate, to standout and connect, to excite and to elicit organize unity can be healthy. Its joyful power to manifest and nourish love enables a couple to be vulnerable and available to each other, enabling them to transcend themselves. Further more, its miraculous power to procreate a third person is essential to humankind. The power of sex can be an epiphany of spirit.

Other Motivations

Past experiences can impede also or encourage us. Clearly, a man who was and still is very dependent on his mother may pursue women who mother him. Or a man who has been controlled and hurt by women can learn to fear and consequently hate dominate women, or submit to and please them. Likewise, a woman who idolizes her father may marry a father figure, or judge all men in light of her "perfect father" If she has been abused by men, she might use sex to manipulate and dominate men, or submit to abuse in a futile attempt to resolve her past problems.

Some people become sexually involved because they never experienced intimacy with anyone on any level—including parents and friends. They transform their basic need to be loved into a quest for genital intimacy. What they really want and need—acceptance, affirmation, and love, they do not get. Although the pain of loneliness is lessened temporarily through genital sex, they soon feel even more lonely and frustrated. Deep within themselves, they desire something more permanent and traanscendent than immediate gratification.

Here is the testimony of a woman who has had little affection from anyone, including her parents and is consequently starved for affection. "No, I'm not proud of myself. I know I have the reputation of being an easy lay. Every man I go out with is prepared for one thing: screwing me. But nobody understands. I don't want to be screwed; I simply want to be loved. I feel ashamed. I guess I'm desperate enough to do almost anything for a little affection."

It is important to realize that our past can also help us. Healthy sex (primary, affective, and genital) education and experiences in childhood and adolescence serve as the foundations for healthy, adult sexuality. Observing healthy marital and sexual models highly influences one's sexual future. Growing up with responsible and good parents who are passionately in love has a positive impact. In short, the past plays a crucial role in our present and future sex lives.

Since sexual behavior is so rewarding, it reinforces itself. Generally, when we behave sexually, the rewards reinforce the behavior or increase the likelihood of behaving sexually once again. Negative reinforcements of avoiding discomfort of whatever type as well as positive reinforcements soon form a strong habit. Behaving sexually with others and/or self can become second nature, or a habit. There is an axiom in sexology that if you don't use it (sex), you'll lose it. In other words, the practice of sexuality increases the likelihood of better sex. If one has a consistent and healthy sex life, sex will get better with aging. In time, one can learn not only better techniques but also how to be more sensitive, gentle, sharing, and loving—how to give and receive more pleasure and fulfillment. As in most things, improvement comes through knowledge and practice.

In the course of years, a married couple can build a storehouse of rich and rewarding memories that they can share and enjoy. Past experiences serve to enrich the present even without consciously calling them forth. The more we "know" each other, the better our lives will be.

There is a plethora of factors that influence one's sexual behavior. For instance, peer pressure, especially for adolescents (or for people who are fixated in or regress to adolescence) can be a strong motivator to have sex. Young adolescents need to be like their peer. The fear of being rejected, isolated, or at least not accepted is powerful. Adolescents and adults who lack a strong sense of identity are apt to go along with the group and the media. A diffused or negative identity makes one very vulnerable to peer pressure as well as to sexual desires.

To be countercultural—to go contrary to the peer group, to mass media, or to the "in" thing—takes inner strength. It is easy to follow the crowd, for then we feel accepted and valued; to be different is difficult. A strong sense of identity is needed to be able to disagree with the main stream. For this reason, the phrase "just say no" is most effective for people who need it the least. People who have a strong sense of identity can say, "yes" to themselves and "no" to behavior that conflicts with their value system. In short, to be fortunate to lack sexual trauma and abuse, to experience healthy role models, and to learn healthy values and sexual standards engenders a healthy sexuality that leads to healthy intimacy.

CHAPTER SIX
NEGATIVE COPING

At various times and degrees, everyone has experienced genital desire. To be human is to be genital. This desire, however, can be frustrating and confusing when gratification is incomplete or not forthcoming. We may feel we are missing something significant. Wanting to give and receive sexually is a natural longing.

In the next two chapters, we will explore and analyze four basic ways of dealing with genitality: negative coping, gratification, positive coping, and integration. In this chapter, we will analyze negative defense mechanisms and physical gratification – common but less than healthy ways of reacting to genital desires.

NEGATIVE DEFENSE MECHANISMS

It is common to defend against natural sexual desires, and it is just as common to satisfy them in less than healthy ways. With good intentions, we can harm ourselves. Think of negative defense mechanisms as processes by which we protect ourselves against unpleasant or anxious feelings that tend to expose unacceptable parts of ourselves. When we cope negatively, we reject certain aspects of ourselves because admitting such experiences would evoke unacceptable pain. Compounding this self-deception is that such defenses are usually unconscious; we do not consciously or willfully choose to use them. Often early in life, we learn to take a less than honest look at our sexual feelings. The good news is that since it is unlikely such defenses are instinctual or innate, they can be unlearned.

Some psychologists suggest that everyone uses defense mechanisms to some extent in order to survive. Ideally, we would wish to avoid employing them, but realistically, most of us at some time have used them. However, how frequently, why, and how we use them highly influence healthy living. The challenge is to become aware of and replace negative coping with positive approaches. To this end, it is helpful to understand what we want to change.

Negative defenses exact a price. They cause us to waste much time and energy in non-productive and repetitious behavior – in trying to be what and who we are not. Moreover, such defenses are not only painful to oneself, but often they are irritating and harmful to others. When we use them, we are less likely to be open to understand and care for others.

A primary reason for using defense mechanisms is to ward off anxiety resulting from unacceptable experiences. For instance, we may defend against genital feelings because we become anxious, ashamed, or guilty when we feel sexual. Sexual feelings evoke unpleasantness, which we hope to avoid. Although immediate unpleasantness may be reduced, we violate ourselves by rejecting an essential part of our personhood. Defense mechanisms are self-defeating. We achieve short-term gains in the reduction of pain, but our long-term losses are much greater and debilitating.

Repression

Repression is a negative defense mechanism that often pervades other defense mechanisms. In fact, many defenses are based on repression. Consider repression as an unconscious effort to exclude certain experiences from conscious awareness. We fool ourselves by not being consciously aware of being unaware. We pretend not to be pretending. Confusing? Yes. This is why persons who constantly repress live in a world of make-believe.

Consider, for example, a person who represses genital feelings. She (or he) does not consciously choose to lie to herself, for her repression is primarily an unconscious process. Although she may have some anxious moments of questioning her sexual self, seldom can she allow herself to reflect on her genitality. If one tells her that she represses, she will feel threatened and consequently become even more defensive. She may innocently deny, anxiously withdraw, vehemently protest, or sincerely intellectualize the truth. Whatever she does, she does not accept and affirm her sexual self.

Why do we unconsciously and automatically expunge experiences from conscious and free awareness? Usually, it is because we have learned and relearned that certain experiences are "unacceptable," make no sense, or are bad in themselves, and that "no good person" would experience them. We can learn early in life that to maintain self-esteem or to be a "valued me," certain experiences must be repressed. To admit such feelings would risk rejection from others or evoke unhealthy guilt (self-rejection).

Consider the repressed woman as a child. If her parent's constantly fostered repression of sex, punishing any sexual expression or discussion, she could learn that her self-esteem depends on being asexual and thus feel compelled to repress sexuality. When sex suddenly and strongly emerges in adolescence, she finds herself poorly prepared to integrate it. After all, she learned to feel that being a good person means being non-sexual. Moreover, her sexual repression may restrict other opportunities for growth. Solitude, for instance, which is essential to healthy growth, might be minimized or filled with noisy thoughts to escape the silence that could evoke her sexuality.

Here are comments of a victim of repression: "I can't stand to be alone. I get these uncomfortable feelings. Yes, I get sexually aroused along with thoughts and fantasies. Then I feel impure and sinful. I don't know what to do. Why me? I try so hard to be pure – to have no sexual feelings and thoughts. But it seems the more I try, the worse it gets."

Repression is costly. When we categorically reject a part of who we are, we pay a price. Repression is a negative reinforcement: What actually happens is that instead of getting rid of an experience, repression increases its strength and promotes pressure for expression. Many costly behaviors come with repressed sexual energy. We may become frustrated, irritable, and angry. We may automatically abstain from intimacy for fear of being sexually aroused, and perhaps use false notions of chastity and celibacy to rationalize our avoidance. We might project or displace our feelings by blaming others for being unchaste, or perhaps achieve some vicarious satisfaction and shaky self-reinforcement by becoming the community or family "sex censor."

Whatever happens, we simply waste time and energy in trying to be what we are not. We become exhausted from going against our natural self. Our freedom is curtailed and our life is violated. Indeed, absolute repression of sexuality is unchaste because it is impure and disrespectful to self and others. Such repression denies human embodiment, making us become "spiritual prunes" – dry and inert.

Denial

Denial is perhaps the most blatant and primitive defense mechanism. It occurs when we refuse to admit that obvious facts or actions even exist. In contrast to repression, denial often deals with external (extrapsychic) interpersonal and environmental activities more than internal (intrapsychic) processes. Denial is rejection of evidence that is obvious to almost anyone except the denying person. A common example is the alcoholic (and often his or her family), who denies this serious disease even when he or she is drunk. An example in the context of sexuality is a woman who dresses and speaks in a sexually provocative manner, and yet completely denies the obvious evidence. Another is a man who treats women as sex objects yet denies sexual exploitation when confronted. People deny because they are unwilling or unable to admit clear evidence. Like all negative defenses, denial is an unconscious process. Confronting denying persons threatens them and often evokes more denial.

Denial often includes more than one person. Such collusion means that two or more people, without consciously agreeing, deny the same reality. For example, a man and a woman do not admit that they are sexually attracted to each other, sensing that such feelings are unacceptable or too much to cope with. Not only do many people deny the same reality, they also pretend that they are not pretending. Spousal, family, friendly, or community collusion only exacerbates and worsens (enables) the reality. Consider the case of a couple who deny their daughter's (or son's) promiscuity. Denying to themselves and each other enables the daughter to continue her sexual activity. More importantly, such denial fails to offer her healthy alternatives.

Rationalization

Rationalization is an irrational way of using rationality. Rationalization is used when one cannot confront the real issue and so attempts to explain and justify feelings or behavior with impersonal, socially acceptable reasons. Instead of taking responsibility for one's acts, the rationalizer tries to minimize the possible effects or to justify the actions. The rationalizer might say: "Almost everyone has premarital or extramarital experiences – why shouldn't I?" As rationalizers, we try to hide behind a general statement instead of reflecting on the true and specific status of our actions. We might say that everything works out in the long run anyhow, so why worry or think about it. Or, as long as we are sincere and honest, our sexual intimacy is okay. Rationalizers fail to realize that sincerity and honesty do not guarantee health.

People who rationalize sex often try to fool themselves about the effects of genital involvement. Take the example of a non-married couple who engages in intercourse. They rationalize their genital involvement, saying that any act done with care is okay. They forget or repress that their care should be a committed and responsible love expressed in the proper time and space. They justify their genital intimacy with a less than healthy theory of care.

Fantasy

Although fantasy can be healthy when in service of health, it is negative when it becomes more important than reality. Fantasies are seductive because they offer the illusion of intimate fulfillment without risk, responsibility, or limits. Fantasy can be creative – and, it can fool us.

Consider the example of a man who nurtures many genital fantasies, seldom approaches people in reality, and fails to make healthy sense of his genitality. Although he feels inferior to women, his compulsive fantasies of overpowering women serve to compensate for his poor sexual identity and self-esteem. Instead of running from reality and hiding in fantasy, he would do better to understand and learn from his true feelings.

Insulation

Insulation occurs when we protect ourselves against hurt and disappointment by not allowing ourselves to care very much. Such "emotional blunting" enables us to remain uninvolved. Instead of being warm and approachable, we keep cool and detached to protect ourselves from emotional and sexual involvement. Insulated persons may not be stimulated genitally or put themselves in situations where this may occur, but they pay the price of being cold and lifeless.

Those who emotionally insulate themselves tend to love "from the neck up." Even though they may be highly competent mentally, emotional expression is highly restricted and curtailed. Being unable to express care highly constricts their life and love.

A woman made the following comments about her husband. "My husband is a good person. You can trust and count on him; he will do anything for me. But he simply cannot share himself. He seems so detached and cold, especially when I ask him how he really feels. Even in sex, which is becoming less frequent, he hides. He seems interested only in quick genital gratification, not in on-going intimacy."

This man may have learned that expressing feelings, including sexual ones, is unmanly, unacceptable, dangerous, or unnecessary. Whatever the reason, he has learned to cope with his feelings by being detached and insulated. It is sad because he is a good person, but a serious consequence of his insulation is that he is losing the art of caring – and is losing his wife. Being boxed in, he will suffocate and lose his spirit. Furthermore, his genital life will continue to dissipate because intimacy needs the expression of love to grow.

Isolation

A similar technique is isolation: cutting oneself off from situations that produce stress. To withdraw freely from a situation can be healthy, but to be compelled to withdraw from any sexually stimulating situation is not healthy.

Take the example of a man who withdraws from women because such involvement evokes sexual feelings. He constantly censors situations and sees only the dangers. In playing "safe," he seldom goes anywhere to have fun and have heterosocial contact, fearing sexual stimulation. Instead of facing and making sense of his sexual feelings, he isolates himself.

Internal isolation involves separating values from activities; actions do not fit words. A man who professes chastity while being sexist is separating theory from practice. The woman who claims sexual openness but refuses to discuss sexual issues is doing the same. The man who preaches love but is afraid of real intimacy lives out of his head, not his experience. These individuals fool themselves and often others, thinking and verbalizing one philosophy while living another.

Regression

Regression describes the tendency to revert to activities – thoughts, judgments, and behaviors– that were characteristics of one's earlier development. When a situation becomes too threatening or overwhelming, we can regress to a level where we feel we have little or no responsibility or to a time when we felt more secure.

For instance, we can regress to (pregenital) childhood because we feel relatively "sexless" and less responsible. An example of this is a woman whose father sexually abused her. Besides repressing her painful feelings, she is anorexic in an attempt to be disembodied and formless so that any evidence of sexuality will "disappear." Furthermore, she dresses and looks like a little girl, instead of a mature, sexual woman. By denying her sexuality and regressing to pre-puberty, she manages to ward off acknowledgment of her painful past. However, the price she pays includes physiological disturbances, lack of intimacy, failure to be herself, and overall frustration and debilitation.

However, some regressive behavior can be healthy. Giggling and kidding about sex, for instance, may be a pleasant way to return to the past, a fun way to explore new feelings. Such regression is a change of pace or a temporary wholesome experience, not a constant way of coping with sex. A husband and wife may take delight in teasing each other as if they were younger than they really are. A group of friends may regress to adolescence in their joking about sexuality. However, people who often regress to adolescence foster immaturity rather than wholesome fun.

Projection

Blaming others for what we think, feel, or do is projection. This defense mechanism maintains self-esteem and adequacy by placing on others our own unacceptable feelings and impulses. For instance, people may accuse others of being unchaste and manipulative as a way of dealing with their unchaste and manipulative feelings. Projection can be difficult for the accused because often they do not know what is occurring. When they are so accused, they may feel guilty for feelings they do not even have, or may become confused and angry with us. Domineering people can make innocent and often dependent persons feel guilty while preserving the perception of their own innocence.

Placing blame on other people or events violates both our own and others' sexuality. Consider, for example, a repressed woman who gets drunk at a party. Under the influence of alcohol, she engages in genital relations. The next morning she uses projection, placing the blame on the alcohol or on the man, or on both. Instead of accepting her responsibility, her projection enables her to maintain her false sense of chastity. Consequently, she feels some degree of self-esteem as a "pure" and guiltless person.

Besides being a matter of dishonesty with oneself, blaming others prevents personal growth. If others really are the reasons for our actions, our freedom to change is highly restricted. We imply that others or events must change in order for us to change. Even if others are at fault, we should not place our freedom to grow on others. After all, they may never change. Besides, we may invest much time and energy in futilely trying to change others rather than ourselves. We can change only our own life.

Displacement

Displacement is the means of emotional switching, the expression from the eliciting person to some other, less risky person or object. For example, instead of expressing anger toward a superior who occasioned it, we can unreflectively dump our anger on a less threatening person – a spouse, friend, child, stranger. Instead of actively confronting the boss, we yell at the innocent checkout clerk, or we drive home recklessly, hollering at anyone in our way.

Displacement is the transferring of emotions from one person to a less threatening person. Some people build up through ongoing repression a "slush fund" of emotion. Then suddenly, they "dump it" on a relatively "safe" person. A man who represses sexuality might build up a slush fund of sexual desires which he periodically displaces (and satisfies) with a prostitute or with masturbation. He momentarily decreases his sexual tension, but fails to deal with his sexuality in a healthy way.

Over-Compensation

A subtle mode of defending oneself against sexuality is over-compensation. Some people engage in genital behavior to make up for feelings of sexual inferiority. Being so-called liberated swingers, they futilely try to establish a sexual identity, but only increase their sense of inadequacy. Such individuals can be deceptive because on the surface they look open and free. Actually, they feel inferior and are too afraid to risk the surrender love requires. Over-compensation is a mask that covers and hides rather than uncovering and sharing ourselves.

Too many men are prone to overcompensate for their lack of authentic sexuality by engaging in genital promiscuity. They are often programmed to be the vanguards of genitality, and to feel that they can somehow find true identity in genital conquests. Unfortunately, increasingly more women are following this mad male model of sexual liberation.

Reaction Formation

Another subtle tactic for dealing with sexuality is reaction formation. This approach replaces unacceptable urges (sexuality) with opposite behaviors and often correspondingly intolerant attitudes. One extreme implies the opposite extreme. For example, sexual prudes often are highly sexual. People all too willing to condemn the sexual activities of others may get satisfaction from their censoring. Reaction formations enable one to maintain a false self-concept of being healthy while at the same time acquiring unhealthy satisfaction.

Some people try to lead celibate lives because they are afraid to face their sexual desires. They equate celibacy with being non-genital; they practice celibacy as a way of coping with unacceptable genital feelings. Such celibacy can also be supported by the culture in that everybody likes "good" people. This does not mean that all celibates employ reaction formations against genitality. Overall, vowed celibates (such as religious sisters, brothers, and priests) are at least as healthy and happy as noncelibates.

Undoing

Undoing is used by people who tend to be perfectionistic, scrupulous, and prone to guilt. For example, scrupulous persons who are obsessed with the sinfulness of feelings and fantasies usually identify feelings with acts. They assume that feeling sexual is the same as behaving sexual. When sexual feelings surface, guilt is intense and frequent. Scrupulous persons can waste enormous amounts of time and energy to undo guilt through confession and penance. Such individuals frequently feel compelled to go through rituals like saying a set of prayers perfectly until they have absolutely cleaned their "moral slate." Instead of facing and integrating sexuality, their compulsive rituals of undoing only bury and exacerbate their repressed sexuality. Soon the submerged sexuality emerges and the corresponding compulsive activities are again triggered. Such scrupulous persons try to be what they are not: nonsexual.

When we genuinely violate sexuality, we should feel guilty — but not primarily so for transgressing a law, but for violating oneself or another. The practice of undoing usually rises from guilt that occurs from breaking unrealistic laws or from an erroneous conscience. The scrupulous ritual of atonement is unhealthy because it comes from a compulsive will. True "at-one-ment" suggests that we become one with ourselves and with one another. It is the opposite of alienation from self and others.

Sympathism

Sympathism is the practice of trying to get others to feel sorry for us and to support us. A woman who feels overwhelmed by sexual feelings and unconsciously feels helpless in dealing with them may employ sympathism. She tries to run from sexual awareness by complaining constantly of her problems. She manipulates people so she can indulge herself in their sympathy and hide from sexual awareness.

Sympathism can be a subtle defense; people believe such a person has no sexual problems or does not think of sexuality — how could such a suffering and sick person be sexual? Complaints, however, usually and quickly turn people off so that the complainers are left with themselves and their sexuality. These people may be compelled to be even "sicker" to pressure others to help them avoid sexual awareness. The therapeutic challenge is to see through this sincere defense to the underlying sexual repression.

Acting Out

Acting out is another defense mechanism that, because it is actively a gratification of need, may not seem so defensive. Acting out refers to the process of dispelling and reducing pressure by acting in a less than healthy manner. Some people who repress genital desires periodically go on sprees of sexual fantasy, pornographic reading, cybersex, masturbation, or sexual intercourse. They may gratify their repressed sexuality several times a year interpersonally or alone.

For some, acting out seems to reduce genital tension and may even evoke guilt that temporarily controls more genital behavior. They get genital desires "out of their system" until they build up again. Acting out is not healthy; it focuses on impulsive or compulsive gratification that is often due to compulsive building up of sexual tension.

The experience expressed by this man bears this out. "I try so hard, and yet I always seem to fail. I really try to keep out any sexual feeling and thoughts, and things seem to be okay for weeks and sometimes even months. But then, bang! I lose all control, and I go on a rampage of gratification. Why does this happen to me?" This well intentioned man is probably repressing his sexuality, and thereby inadvertently building up pressure to satisfy himself.

GRATIFICATION

We satisfy genital needs directly for many reasons. If we are tense, lonely, or bored, sexual satisfaction lessens the stress. It can make us feel like something, someone, and somebody who is fulfilled. It can purge discomfort and give a feeling of peace. Indeed it can, but only temporarily.

We have seen that genital behavior evokes pleasure. However, pursuing only pleasure can be unhealthy or at least "not healthy" — that is, while seeking pleasure is "normal," as an isolated endeavor it does not foster wholistic growth. This so-called normal, physical emphasis on sex is mad and bad because it treats self and others as simply physical beings; this violates our personal integrity. To identify the human person as mainly genital is to debase our own and the other's dignity.

We have also noted that single life, unlike marital life, does not offer the commitment, time, and place necessary to foster healthy sexual growth. Since genital behavior calls for marital commitment, single people who engage in genital relations can eventually feel cheated, frustrated, tense, unfulfilled, or resentful when the promise of love is not kept. Of course, married persons who do not nurture their commitment can feel just as hurt and empty, often moreso.

Extramarital sex can be considered "normal" in that such behavior is frequently practiced and is socially accepted or tolerated; it may also reduce tension and afford pleasure. But, mores are not the same as morals. Objectively, extramarital relations are neither healthy nor good. Certainly, all extramarital sex is not primarily or exclusively selfish. It can be a sincere expression of love that is centered on another. When two persons are in love, they truly (without exploitation) desire the union and life that genital sex offers. It is difficult to abstain from genital relations when authentic love pervades the relationship.

Nevertheless, a challenge is to abstain from genital involvement while fostering love. Although abstinence can be frustrating and sometimes even seem unnatural, it is the better way. To be sure, premarital and extramarital genital behavior have meaning, but they remain less than healthy because they impede on-going psychological and spiritual growth. If this is true, what can we do with our sexual desires whether they include or exclude love?

CHAPTER SEVEN
POSITIVE COPING AND INTEGRATION

Many people learn only two ways of dealing with sexual desires: repression or physical gratification. This is not much of a choice, for both fall short of being healthy. However, there are healthy ways to cope with and integrate sexuality. Certain psychological and spiritual strategies can reduce stress, increase freedom and control, and facilitate healthy growth. We will consider the psychological approaches first.

SUPPRESSION

Suppression, like repression, is the checking of an experience, but suppression, unlike repression, involves conscious awareness of an experience that is kept from overt expression. Suppression is a "no" that is based on a more fundamental "yes." When we choose to suppress sexuality, we begin by freely affirming feelings and sexual desires. Instead of being an automatic and unconscious act, suppression involves self-affirmation and free choice.

Ideally, we should admit all experiences to ourselves, though not necessarily expressing them to others or acting on them. When we feel sexual, we can admit and affirm that experience. Suppression, in contrast to repression, increases the alternatives for more healthy behavior.

To suspend or bracket thoughts and feelings is one alternative. For instance, the suspension of genital feelings is appropriate while listening, studying, teaching, or performing a task; it provides the necessary discipline needed to focus freely on the matter at hand without disruptions. Having neither desire nor time to reflect on genital feelings, they are bracketed, put on the shelf. When we urgently desire genital expression, it may not be a good time for oneself or the other, an appropriate place may not be available, or the commitment may be absent. In this case, we say "yes" to the feelings, then choose not to focus on them. We refuse to give them attention, thereby lessening their strength. (Attention, especially obsessiveness, usually reinforces feelings.)

Sometimes suppression is easy; at other times it is difficult. One's psychological state highly influences the degree of ease or difficulty. For instance, someone who is lonely, sexually desirous, tired, and stressed will have more difficulty with suppression than one who feels connected, alert, comfortable, and without genital urges. Sometimes mortification and always discipline are necessary.

Mortification

To many people, mortification elicits visions of painful and meaningless penance, self-punishment, or pathological asceticism. However, mortification is sometimes necessary for suppression and overall health as well. Mortification also is a "no" in the service of a "yes." Mortification, literally meaning "to make dead," is healthy when it fosters growth. Healthy mortification suggests that sometimes death is necessary to have life.

Consider this scene: A man who desires genital relations with his fiancée, but freely chooses to mortify his feelings. He first affirms his genital feelings, then says "no" to or mortifies the genital expression of his love. Instead of withdrawing from himself and his beloved, he rejects genital expression while remaining present, with his desires, to his future wife. He remains sexual, but freely refuses to engage in genital behavior. This man says: "Yes, I want very much to express my love in genital relations, but I do not think it would be best for either of us at this time." Such mortification can be very difficult and uncomfortable, but it is a "death" that promotes a life of love.

Mortification may seem old-fashioned or masochistic, but actually it is quite congruent with research on adult development and spiritual formation. Although the word mortification is not used, most developmental psychologists readily agree that growth periodically involves pain and letting go of both negative and positive experiences. Often, one must endure losses to achieve gains. Classical and contemporary spirituality also affirms the need to purge both negative and positive experiences (e.g., to move from one level of development to another). Mortification is not out-dated; it is a necessary approach to wholistic growth.

Discipline

Suppression and mortification demand discipline. Although discipline is often equated with regression or restriction, it is actually the basis of freedom. Many people find discipline difficult because in childhood they had almost all their needs satisfied. Moreover, our culture promotes immediate satisfaction instead of delayed gratification. The person who has always gotten anything he or she wanted (food, TV, toys, movies, music, money, etc.) may find it more difficult to suppress sex than a person who did not have needs satisfied so readily. Lack of discipline leads to entitlement, and doing whatever we want. Discipline begins in early childhood. To embrace it later in life is difficult, but still possible.

Discipline is both popular and unpopular today. On the one hand, discipline is glorified as a necessary condition for physical well-being and intellectual and career development. On the other hand, mass media, culture, and individuals promote immediate gratification and a general flight from discomfort. Living for the moment or in the most comfortable situation is the message. Such a philosophy and psychology encourage narcissistic self-gratification.

As embodied persons, our freedom is both limited and dynamic. Responding to the realities of time, space, genetics, anatomy, physiology, culture, education, environment, religion, and other factors, discipline molds — limits and facilitates — our abilities and behavior. It controls and hones our embodiment to enable us to express ourselves as freely as possible. Without discipline, an individual can easily succumb to immediate gratification or to sexist and hedonistic scripts. Discipline helps us to control and abstain from forces that impede free choice.

From Repression To Suppression

Problems can emerge when one moves from repression to suppression. During this transitional time, it is not rare to see a person act almost the opposite of past repressive behavior. Consider a woman who repressed her sexual feelings in early adolescence and young adulthood. In her thirties or later, she becomes conscious of and has opportunities for sexual involvement. After many years, she now suddenly finds herself confronted with intense genital desires and fantasies. She may feel confused and fascinated with her newly emergent genital self. Instead of being defensive about or unaware of sex, she shows flexibility and vitality, thinks about and wants to talk about sex, and is tempted to experiment with her new feelings. Being accustomed with her old "sexless" self, her friends' expectations conflict with the woman's new sexual self. Some of them may pressure her to be her old self, criticizing her, asking her what is wrong, alienating her. Others may encourage her to gratify her desires, steering her toward situations where genital gratification can occur. All these people err. They would do better making themselves available to help her accept and take time to learn healthy ways to cope with her changing self.

SUBLIMATION

Sublimation, meaning to raise or to elevate feelings, refers to the redirecting of energy from one activity to another that is judged to be culturally, socially, physically, functionally, aesthetically, or spiritually "higher" or better. Sublimation, like suppression, is an acceptance of feelings that we choose not to gratify in behavior. Rather than holding in check as with suppression, the one who sublimates re-channels or invests energy into an activity that is in harmony with his or her values. Instead of directly satisfying genital desires, this tactic invests genital energy in activities that are congruent with and promote healthy and good living. Of course, if one has immature or unhealthy values, sublimation as well as suppression will be difficult or seem senseless.

Sublimation begins by suppressing sexual feelings (which means affirming and controlling them), then freely choosing to direct energy toward actions that promote healthy living. A frequently used approach in the past was to "get busy," especially in manual labor or athletics. This kind of simple sublimation is still useful and helpful, but there are other ways as well. For example, we can re-channel sexual energy into intellectual pursuits such as studying and reading, or direct it toward aesthetic and creative activity. When suppressed and invested in love, sublimated sexuality can promote healthy relationships. Indeed, it is possible to sublimate genital sex while remaining in and promoting a relationship of love. With practice and time, sublimation can become largely habitual.

One woman describes her use of sublimation: "When I feel real sexual, I can do several things. Sometimes I clean my room; at other times, I just get involved in a book or a TV program. When it's really intense, I do some strenuous activity like running or cleaning my apartment. I find that calling a friend also helps."

ANTICIPATION

Anticipation refers to the practice of predicting what is likely to occur. As its etymology indicates, anticipation suggests that one foresees what will probably happen and plans a course of action that will prevent negative consequences. For instance, some women know that at certain times they will desire more affection, affirmation, and understanding than other times. They also knows from past experience that when they drink alcohol or are tired, they have less control and are more vulnerable to satisfying their sexual desires. They know that, given these and other conditions, they must take special care of themselves. Consequently, accepting a dinner invitation from a charming and sexually manipulative man at his apartment would be foolish if a woman wants to avoid sexual involvement. Likewise, an engaged couple who feel vulnerable must take extra precautions – both individually and together — if they want to safeguard chastity. They know what can occur.

Effective anticipation depends on knowing oneself. How do I feel now? How have I (and others) acted in past situations like this? What is likely to occur? Instead of falling into negative defense mechanisms, such questioning helps us to learn from our present feelings and past experiences in order to ensure a better future. Perfect judgments and courses of action are not guaranteed, but self-awareness and learning significantly increase one's freedom of choice.

For example, anticipation is one way to deal with compulsive masturbating. For instance, knowing the times of the month and day when one is more vulnerable can be helpful. Alcoholics Anonymous has an acronym called "HALT." It is a reminder that when one is Hungry (in whatever way), Angry, Lonely, or Tired, to be careful. This advice is relevant not only to alcoholism, but to any problem. Indeed, we must halt sometimes: stop, step back, think, and take measures to deal with our vulnerability.

Anticipation calls for humility— the acceptance of being on earth and of being less than completely free. Being humble does not mean putting ourselves down or being weak; rather it is lifting ourselves up to self-awareness. Humility is the recognition that we are neither in perfect control nor can we orchestrate all feelings and behaviors in our self and others. Although sometimes feelings seem to have a life of their own exercise choice and control within our limitations.

People who think they can always control their feelings and behaviors or handle those of another are fools. They deceive themselves, assuming that they have more power than the facts bear out. Self-deception is often rationalization for unacceptable behavior. Consider, for example, a celibate man in love with a woman. If he thinks he can spend considerable personal time with her without being moved to physical intimacy, he is arrogant or naïve. Such pride will only lead to trouble. This is not to say that he be paranoid, withdrawn, or fearful. He should be humble in accepting that he cannot control everything. He can anticipate situations when and where he or she will be vulnerable and plan to use healthy coping strategies. Anticipation, of course, can be negative. Expecting the worst lays the foundations for self-fulfilling prophecies. Repression, low self-esteem, or a puritanical conscience engender jaded, narrow expectations. Open acceptance of the present and learning from the past lead to a vital, humble, and serene approach to life. Positive anticipation presupposes and fosters the wisdom and courage that engender healthy sexuality.

FRIENDS

Friends and trustworthy persons can be helpful in coping with and resolving long- or short-term crises. Disclosure of sexual feelings and dilemmas with a friend can help in many ways. First, being genuinely listened to and understood invariably increases our well-being. Second, getting our inside feelings out decreases stress, conserves energy, and increases hope and freedom. Third, we feel less unique and alone by sharing; we discover that the boat we are on is not empty but very crowded. Instead of being self-sufficient and isolated, we share with another. Instead of feeling alien, we realize we are decidedly human.

"For some time, I've had these sexual desires and fantasies," comments one woman. "I sort of knew that it was okay, and yet I felt frustrated, confused, and alone. Although I knew better, I still felt that few people felt like I did, or that no one would understand, or that I would be criticized for being weird or wrong. Finally, after mustering up the courage to share with an older friend, I felt more human and at peace. Even though she didn't say much, I felt normal, that I could work things out. I feel much better now."

When a mature friend is unavailable, a counselor may help. A competent counselor offers confidentiality, security, acceptance, understanding, and the help to resolve and improve. If progress is not discerned and experienced, acquire a new counselor.

Another approach is to join a fellowship. People with similar interests, problems, and challenges meet regularly to help one another within and outside group meetings. Compassionate and confidential fellowships give support, courage, and suggestions for improvement.

With or without professional help, we can help one another. People who have gone or are going through similar experiences can help one another. It is not necessary to feel alone or discouraged; we can gain the courage and insight to change for the better.

As one woman noted about her group experience, "I never dreamed that so many people felt like I do. I thought that no one could feel as confused and hurt as I. Then I listened to the stories and feelings of others in my group, how they managed to feel better, freer, and okay. The group listened to my experiences of being sexually abused; they really understood. They gently and firmly helped me come out of denial; they supported me as I expressed my anger and fear.

"Because of them, I came out of my confusion, not feeling guilty or ashamed. Having been there themselves, they gave me a special gift of empathy. And, no, they didn't treat me with kid gloves, but they were compassionate and understanding. Now I am happy to say that I've accepted what happened to me, that I'm beginning to forgive my father and mother. What's more, I'm helping others to come out of their black holes to see and enjoy the light."

INTEGRATION

Genital sex, we have seen, has much more than a physical meaning; it can have a direct and positive influence on our psychological and spiritual life. Therefore, it should not be regarded as an enemy or impediment, but rather as a friend, a help in living a healthy single or married life. Indeed, genital feelings can evoke and promote personal integration.

The etymological meaning of integration – to make whole – gives an important clue to its sexual application, particularly in light of the wholistic perspective stressed here. Integration denotes the process of renewing or restoring an *integer*, a whole.

Clinically, integration involves experiencing the whole from which the parts emerge. Integrating genital feelings begins by experiencing genitality as part of and a revelation of the whole person. While genital feelings, fantasies, and behavior are physical functions, they also manifest and reveal something about ourselves and others as integral (whole) people. Healthy people learn to experience the whole person partially revealed in genitality. If we overemphasize the genital, we fragment ourselves and others.

Respect literally means "to see again" or to take a second look. A key to integration is to see genital sex as a manifestation of the whole person. Such creative seeing enables us to appreciate the deeper dimensions of self and others. Instead of separating genital feelings from the whole self, or seeing them merely as biological functions, we experience sex as an invitation to wholeness.

"When I'm sexually attracted to a man, I make an effort not just to focus on sex," comments one woman. "I look at how he carries himself, speaks, and behaves. If I'm really interested, I find out about his character and values. I want to know how he thinks about important issues — and, me as well. I want to know if he is a jerk or a real man. Of course, if I were not sexually attracted to him in the first place, I might have passed him by."

She is right. Our sexual feelings invite us to the process of integration. Sex might be characterized as a "rupture" in everyday life that breaks through the forgetfulness and busyness of normal living to help us respect and fully appreciate ourselves and others. Specifically, sex says: "Stop! Respect reality — take a second look at yourself and the other. Don't take people for granted." However, what we see depends on how we look.

We have seen that attitudes co-determine the meaning of reality, and consequently how we feel and behave. For example, an artist employing his aesthetic perspective, is less likely to regard a nude woman as a genital partner; he will see her aesthetically. His "aesthetic eyes" appreciate her whole being — physical, psychological, and spiritual. His painting will try to capture the woman's beauty, uniqueness, personality, and spirit. If his painting is good, it will help viewers to deepen their appreciation of all women. Likewise, authentic single or married lovers are not apt to identify themselves or others with a physical part (breasts, legs, genitals) or a function (wife, friend, lover); rather, they are more inclined to experience these parts and functions as expressions and affirmations of the whole human being. Such persons are authentically chaste: They can appreciate without selfishness, manipulation, or exploitation. A chaste posture is pure — a respectful and integral presence to reality.

Gender

In an earlier chapter, I proposed that women are more disposed than men to seek a deeper satisfaction than the physical when they feel sexual. They place genital sex in the light of tenderness, affection, and care, and they tend to hear more clearly the call for a permanent and faithful commitment. Nevertheless, men also can respond to the sacredness of genitality and be more sensitive and caring.

In our Western culture, however, men are more likely than women to isolate genital desires in terms of physical satisfaction. When genital desires incite a man to "take a second look," his experience depends largely on his attitude toward women. If he experiences a woman as an object for sexual satisfaction, he will identify her with her physical being, minimize or deny her wholeness, and consequently long to use her for selfish satisfaction.

The following remarks represent an immature attitude toward women.

"Personally, I'm a boob man. Breasts really turn me on. The bigger and firmer, the better. Of course, I don't mind nice legs and rears either. A nice face helps, too. God knew what he was doing when he made breasts. They really turn me on." This man focuses parts of a woman, not her whole person. His crass and arrogant attitude betrays his immaturity and lack of respect for women — as well as for himself.

What would it be like to be a man who is genitally attracted to a woman's breasts? What does he experience? Does he only or primarily see breasts? If so, his experience is neither healthy nor good, for no such independent reality as "breasts" exists, only a person who is and has breasts. This man separates and represses the psychological and especially spiritual dimensions of the woman and of himself. Consequently, he impoverishes what he and she are and can be. He lacks respect for himself. Moreover, he diminishes his integrity by failing to appreciate sexuality (his own and another's) as an expression of the whole person.

The healthier stance for this man would be to regard the woman and himself psychologically and spiritually as well as physically. Instead of fragmenting her being, separating her breasts from her personhood or maximizing the meaning of physical sex — he could respect more integrally her breasts as expressions of her personhood, womanhood, femininity, beauty, life, nurturance, and care. His desires could help him to appreciate her as a person, beautiful, intelligent, resourceful, assertive, a mystery to behold. Relating as a whole human being, he would then claim and manifest a sexuality that is healthy and good.

Fantasies

Let us consider sexual fantasies in light of integration. For instance, a man may discover himself day dreaming about genital sex. What does he experience? Does he imagine making love without weight, smell, touch, taste, — a senseless love? Does he focus on genitals apart from the person or a person with genitals? How real is his sexual fantasy? Does he fantasize about lovemaking as one euphoric state without limits, fears, and clumsiness? Does he want the pleasure of sex and the perfection of intimacy without the limits and responsibilities of real, committed sex? Him fantasies of and desires to make loving sex are natural, but his challenge is to keep in touch with the whole of reality.

We should pay attention to what our sexual fantasies tell us about ourselves and about our relationships with people. What kind of person am I in fantasies as contrasted with my everyday self? Am I assertive and adventurous in sexual fantasies and docile and timid in everyday life? How do I act in fantasy? Fantasies can help us become more aware of our desires and views about sex. Through them we can learn about ourselves to promote growth rather than immaturity or fixation.

To do this we must claim, name, and explain our sexual feelings. However, this is not an invitation to cultivate and promote genital feelings and fantasies. Rather, honest and truthful acceptance of spontaneous feelings and fantasies can help us to understand what is happening. Genital feelings give more than a physical message; fantasies reveal more than mere genitality. Respect enables us to be open to the various meanings revealed in genitality. Because sex is an articulation of the whole person, it can be an opportunity to learn from and about oneself.

This woman has a healthy attitude toward her fantasies. "I try to learn about myself from my fantasies. Sometimes, my fantasies are too physical. This tells me that I am capable of being less than I want to be. I try to bring love into sex. Usually, I imagine being in an affectionate relationship where the man is thoughtful and gentle. And I am not only a recipient of his affection; I respond in kind. Genital sex may not even occur. When it does, it is part of the whole experience. Such fantasies tell me what I really want — a respectful and gentle love, a true sharing. Though mere physical sex can be exciting, it leaves me empty. I have learned that it's not what is best for me, nor what I really need and want."

Positive Amplification

Positive amplification is also helpful in promoting respect and integration. Instead of repressing, escaping, or gratifying genital feelings, amplification involves extending, deepening, and enriching fantasies, dreams, and reality. It does not countenance willful activation or encouragement of genital feelings; it demands respect for genital impulses as parts of one's whole self. Negative amplification, however, could involve stimulation or promotion of genital desires for immediate satisfaction. To look for the spiritual within the genital is helpful for maintaining a wholistic perspective. For example, we should not see only an erect penis.

An erect penis is not an experiential reality; but only a man who has an erect penis is real. Likewise, there is no such reality as an "erect clitoris," only a woman who has an erect clitoris. The physical changes in genitalia can indicate that the whole person is standing out, moving toward, yearning for, and is receptive of intimacy with another. They can express the fact that one's whole being, not just genital being, is seeking intimacy and interpersonal fulfillment. Genital yearning is a distinct way of uncovering the transcendent dynamic of being human: desire for union with another.

Of course, we can refuse the call to integration and focus exclusively on the physical dimension of genitality. A price is paid when we maximize the physical and seek immediate pleasure. Purging the spiritual and failing to respect and promote wholeness frustrate spiritual growth and therefore healthiness.

Too many of us neither believe in ourselves nor trust our spiritual selves; consequently, we dissociate rather than integrate our genital sexuality. Instead of fostering the unity of love and sex, we maintain a duality between the two or focus exclusively on genitality. Marital sex can be just as or spiritless as nonmarital recreational sex. Moreover, it probably has more negative consequences within marriage than outside of it.

Healthy amplification incorporates creative control. Instead of habitually satisfying, repressing, or blindly restricting fantasies and feelings, the individual uses discipline to follow the truth of his or her genitality. This control is not violent — it does not treat the genital self as an enemy. Rather, it involves "being with"; that is, approaching the genital self as a friend. The relaxed discipline and attentive freedom of creative control enables a person to test limits, expand horizons, and deepen values.

Sometimes genital feelings can be so strong and loud that they "silence" the messages of other feelings. For instance, a man may so intensely yearn to be genitally intimate with a woman that he loses control of himself. He treats himself and the woman only as genital beings. Creative listening would help him to hear more than just genital feelings. Within the clamor and confusion of genital feelings is the drive to become whole with another. Are we willing and able to listen for the whisper of spiritual longings within our genitality?

"I hear what you're saying", one man confessed, "but when I get horny, it's really difficult to appreciate the whole person. I think you're right about responding to the whole person, but it's as if my genital desires take over. I guess that's when I have to get some distance. In a sense, I have to sober up. I have to make a strong effort to remind myself that the woman is not a sex object for my pleasure. She has feelings and values just like my sister or mother. It helps to remind myself that she is just as human as they are."

Instead of concentrating on only a part of a person, we can be open to another's integrity (wholeness) and experience his or her dignity (worth) as well as our own. This creative seeing involves cutting through the surface to regard and appreciate sex as a revelation of the whole person and as a yearning for communion. To interpret genital yearnings as biological drives alone, is a one-sided perception. It is also a violation of the dignity of human personhood, of our spiritual or communal dimension.

Imagine a man who is sexually attracted to a girl who finds himself admiring her physical appearance. Instead of identifying her with her physicality, thinking of how "to make out" or "to make her," he can amplify his perception and thereby appreciate her, even though he may never speak to her. For instance, he may look at the way she presents herself — the way she dresses and expresses herself. What does her body language say? Is she stiff or relaxed, aloof or friendly, sad or glad, scared or confident? It is important that he see her as a member of the same community of humankind as he. Such creative reflection can help the man become intimate with her even though she remains a stranger. Instead of taking a one-sided look, he regards her more wholly and realistically.

Imagine a woman who fantasizes about making love with a man. Instead of blocking her feelings prematurely, she can amplify her fantasies to see where they lead her. Instead of stopping her fantasy short at romance, physical involvement, or orgasm, she might consider what is likely to happen after sex. Do he and she suddenly disappear? Is everything all over and forgotten? Is there a future? If so, what kind? What real difference does such intimacy make? Will it make her more mature? Better? Healthier? More loving? More committed? What are the real consequences likely to be? Such healthy amplification involves an extension of the possible consequences of fantasy and links the fantasy with reality. It makes fantasy more real.

HUMOR

Humor can help us to cope with and integrate sexuality. Humor is usually associated with fun and playful situations, with free and easy times, with experiences that are not demanding and stressful. Indeed, humor can be a healthy part of sexuality. To appreciate how men and women respond differently to the same situations can at times be humorous. Affective kidding, bantering, and flirting, can be fun. Genital play often includes humor.

Indeed, any type of sex can be serious or without humor, but sex often lends itself to humor. Sex invites us to loosen and open up, to be zestful and light. In humor, we are on the same plane regardless of our education and socioeconomic status. Like sex, humor brings us together; it fosters intimacy in a safe situation. In humor, we get close to each with safe and appropriate boundaries.

Humor can not only be a part of sexuality, it can also help us to abstain from inappropriate sexual behavior. Humor can bring sex into a perspective that militates against fixating on sex. It loosens the grip that sex may have on us so that we are freer to manage our desires. Smiling or laughing lessens the intensity and urgency of sex. Humor invites us to dance with people rather than using them as a means for gratification.

In a certain sense, humor can be a spring board to the divine. It can open us to more than is initially seen, to a reality that is both part of and more than ourselves. Humor can evoke enthusiasm for earthly ways of being connected to God. Humor taps into a reality that strengthens, liberates, and heals.

PRAYER

Some people consider prayer a foolish endeavor — an illusion. Authentic prayer, however, is a realistic and practical way to help us become our sexual selves. Because spirituality is the paramount dynamic of integration, prayer is the primary way to maintain, nourish, and facilitate integration. To pray when pressured to engage in or while involved in sex fosters integration, engenders a wholistic perspective, and gives power. Prayer is not pie in the sky; it is an effective approach supported by empirical and clinical research.

Prayer is connecting with God, our uncreated creator, sustainer, motivator, and destiny. At anytime, but especially when we feel powerless and unable to manage, prayer helps. God gives us strength to maintain and promote our spiritual life.

Through prayer, we realize that we are more than individuals, that we are in communion with others and God. We affirm that our sustaining source of healthy and happy living is brotherhood and sisterhood in, with, and through God. Prayer encourages us to broaden our vision and to allow the spiritual to affect us. To cooperate with a power that is greater than ourselves, to live with a Transcendent Presence that helps and heals, is essential to wholistic living.

Besides explicitly sacred practices like liturgy, meditation, and personal and group prayer, an orientation of love is vital. To live a life of love helps us to admit our dependence on the Divine and to keep a wholistic perspective. Being mindful of the Transcendent allows affairs and encourages us to see and respond to sexuality in healthy ways.

Although prayer contains the possibility of miracles, more likely, God grants us the grace and serenity that enables us to accept, understand, and cope with the challenges, frustrations, and opportunities of sexuality. Those who do not pray rob themselves of the most effective source for becoming healthy (sexual) persons. It is foolish not to pray. Prayer is our reason for being.

CHAPTER EIGHT
PURSUING ABSTINENCE

Before the social and religious revolutions of the 1960's, sexual (genital) abstinence was encouraged and rewarded, and non-marital sexual behavior was forbidden or kept secret. Sexual feelings and fantasies were likely to be controlled and often repressed, or they were ambivalent temptations that could lead to guilt or damnation. Our times, however, have changed.

Some might say that instead of following a Jansenistic script of affective and sexual restriction, we have now learned to dance to a post-modern tune of sexual expression and gratification. This new model of sexuality has offered more possibilities, some good ones and others not so good. For instance, women are relatively freer from sexist obstacles and freer for functional and personal growth. More men are exploring the possibilities of androgyny and intimacy.

Yet, there is evidence that we have moved toward the opposite end of the sexual continuum. Instead of extra-marital sex being symptomatic of mental illness, moral depravity, or a one-way ticket to hell, it is often construed as healthy, good, and perhaps a ticket to heaven. Instead of being a source of guilt and shame, sex is seen as an individual choice that can increase self-esteem and satisfaction. Particularly in mass media, abstinence is seldom seen as a wise choice, but often as a sign of being less than free or of a sad state of affairs.

Both the old and new ways have arguably engendered negative consequences. Both shameful repression and licentious gratification fail to promote true freedom and health. Our contention has been that a more balanced model than rigid restriction or blatant expression is needed. Another alternative, sexual abstinence, is offered, but for different reasons than given perhaps in the past or present.

Indeed, few people find abstinence easy, for we have seen that sexual desire is a powerful and essential experience of humankind. Sexual abstinence is not a popular topic or practice; in fact, it is counter cultural. My goal is to show how abstinence, beyond preventing untoward consequences like sexually transmitted diseases and pregnancy, can foster freedom and health. How do you look at sexual abstinence? What is your understanding? Do you harbor old assumptions of repression or strict avoidance? Or do you have new attitudes of expression and gratification? Does abstinence make sense or nonsense, or both? How we—you and I—construe abstinence will highly influence how we judge (self and others) and practice or abstain from abstinence. We will see that abstinence is not only important for single and vowed religious persons, but also for married persons.

Although the focus is on sexuality, the principles of abstinence can usually be applied to any activity. As a response to our culture of opulence and indulgence, abstinence can be a useful strategy to cope with the questionable assumption that more is better. The addiction to "more"—"over" eating, drinking, watching, computing, playing, and working—clearly impedes health. My wish is that presenting the pros and cons of abstinence will help any person of any age to make freer and healthier choices. So, let us reflect on the meaning of abstinence.

Healthy, normal, and unhealthy ways of responding to sexuality have been discussed. A thesis has been that everyone should strive to cultivate all modes of sexuality with the caveat of genital behavior being healthy only in marriage. If this ideal is to be pursued, then abstinence becomes a crucial issue. The topic of this chapter is abstinence – an old practice that is being renewed.

ABSTINENCE

What is abstinence and how does it work? An initial response is to state what abstinence is not. Healthy abstinence is not repressive, rigid, or deceptive, but it involves freedom and awareness. It is not an attempt to reject what is, namely sexual desires. Neither is abstinence similar to projection, displacement, reaction formation, or rationalization. Rather than distorting reality, abstinence affirms reality and responds accordingly. While abstinence is an avoidance of direct gratification, it is a response to sexual needs. We will see that abstinence is more like suppression—an awareness of but a decision not to act on feelings.

Abstinence, which is derived from the Latin *ab* (away from, against) and *tenere* (to hold), literally means "hold away from" one's self, or to refrain from behavior that directly gratifies one's needs. Abstinence involves a choice to detach from certain behaviors. "Holding away from" means that we "hold" (*tenere*) or connect with sexuality as well as keeping "away from" (*ab*) gratification.

Abstinence is taking a stand that includes both a "yes" and a "no." When we abstain, we say yes (*tenere*) to our sexual desires, and we decide to say no (*ab*) to certain behaviors. Unlike repression or other unhealthy coping reactions, the no of abstinence is a detachment from certain behaviors in service of attachment, attainment, and connection. For example, the recovering alcoholic must say no to or abstain from alcoholic consumption in order to say yes to recovery. Likewise, it is necessary to say no to the pleasures of sexual gratification in order to say yes to the value of abstinence.

In short, abstinence presupposes and is based on a conscious awareness of our needs, desires, and thoughts. The free refusal to act on sexual feelings is healthy when it is in service of a way better than sexual gratification. To reiterate: Saying "no" to sexual gratification (or any gratification) presupposes a "yes."

To abstain, we must be willing and able. Willingness involves choice that implies values. Simply stated: If we have no reason to say no, i.e., if we lack a yes, it is very different to abstain. Actually, it makes little sense and in some respects is stupid. To abstain from sex calls for better sense than gratification.

Opting for abstinence also presupposes the ability to choose. Unfortunately, for whatever reasons, there may be people who are unable to choose abstinence. They may be so mired in sexual addiction that they have little freedom. Or when under the influence of alcohol or other drugs, they may be unable to exercise free choice. To be sure, it is the responsibility of a person who is combating pathology, addiction, habit, or immaturity to try to achieve the ability to choose. We are simply saying that all people are not the same. Some people are freer because they have the ability, motivation, and opportunity to achieve abstinence. Since there are so many variables that make it easier or harder to practice abstinence, it is dangerous and unfair to project one's own standards and feelings onto someone else.

A Continuum of Abstinence

Abstinence is necessary to keep personal and social order. If we satisfied all of our needs, chaos would result and civilization would crumble. Complete devotion to a pleasure principle would lead to personal and social anarchy. However, not all abstinence is the same. One way of looking at abstinence is on a continuum—from mild to moderate to severe.

The degree of abstinence can be determined by the consequences that would occur without it. For example, severe or extreme abstinence would be necessary for a heroin addict because without abstinence there is no recovery, and without recovery, dire consequences occur. Likewise, a pedophile must abstain from personal and vicarious contact with children. There are no exceptions. Absolute abstinence is necessary for recovery.

A moderate degree of abstinence is called for in everyday living. Abstaining from "too much"—eating and drinking, television, computer, work, play, and sleep—is necessary for optimal functioning. Otherwise, life gets out of balance and eventually causes negative consequences. Diet, which etymologically means a way of living, is necessary for balance and health.

Mild abstinence often involves activities that we take for granted, like abstaining from speaking too loudly, walking in people's way, dressing inappropriately, and staring. With little or no effort, most of us abstain from rude and intrusive behavior, and obnoxious people usually receive negative feedback. In short, life is permeated with abstinence.

Applying this framework to sexuality, severe or absolute abstinence is imperative with sex addictions. Not only must sex offenders abstain from certain sexual activities but also from lust and desires to act out. Sex offenders must also learn to abstain from fostering fantasies that are related to their offenses. Although we cannot control feelings, desires, and fantasies that spontaneously occur, we can abstain from nurturing and fostering them.

Moderate sexual abstinence may involve refraining from pornography or sexist language and behavior. Although abstaining from media and places that present human beings as sex objects is not as serious as abstaining from sexual behavior with minors, it nevertheless is needed for healthy behavior. While pornography and sexist behavior may be common, they are not healthy. At best, such behaviors are immature or normally mad.

Moderate to mild abstinence may involve a refusal to support sexist TV programs. Such a stand may seem puritanical and ludicrous, yet support of sexist media is less than healthy. To abstain from immodest dress and behavior may also be a form of mild abstinence. Even in marriage sexual abstinence is not rare. Because of many personal and situational factors, married persons do not always satisfy their desires. Respect for self and other often calls for abstinence.

THE SENSE OF ABSTINENCE

We have emphasized the importance of the presence of spiritual components like mystery, ecstasy, and connection in sexual experiences. For instance, mystery is always present in sex. Knowledge of the other (as well as one's self) is inexhaustible and, at least implicitly, awe-inspiring. Even though mystery and awe may be subtle or repressed, they are still powerfully alluring and potentially reverential. Sex demands that we acknowledge that we are infinitely more than mere physical beings. Something unique, special, and sacred is present. This is one reason why rape is so despicable and why prostitution is a lowering of one's self. For such reasons, it is wise to abstain from sex that violates our spirit.

Sex is transcendent in seeking connection. By nature, sex goes beyond itself. It moves toward unification, co-creation, and procreation.

Sex seeks "the more than" (one's self). In sex, we desire to join, to be in union with. So, when we repress the spiritual, sex becomes much less than it can be, moving toward narcissism and less toward wholesome union. Paradoxically, the sacred sense of sex can motivate us to indulge in or to abstain from sex.

We have seen that having sex is powerfully alluring and meaningful. The more overt and common motivations include pleasure, stress reduction, fun, ecstasy, enjoyment, as well as the more idiosyncratic and personal reasons like power, past experiences, and issues of self-esteem, loneliness, and addiction. The more covert and paramount dynamic of sex is spiritual—the desire for completion in union with another. To achieve healthy abstinence, we must honor and respond to the sacred in sex. Healthy abstinence occurs when we honor the spirit of sex.

Perhaps more than ever before, it is difficult to abstain from anything, particularly sexuality. To abstain means to go against much of what is normal, against the *Zeitgeist*. It takes courage to be countercultural, and when we go against or do things differently than the majority, flack is usually evoked. In other words, abstinence can evoke and provoke uncomfortable consequences. To say "no" when many are saying "yes" can evoke criticism, retribution, and alienation instead of than approval, admiration, and support.

To abstain means to go against many mass media models. It means listening to a different voice than that of individualism and gratification. The ethic "what makes me feel good is good" or "it is my right to do what I want" has to be transgressed. When we abstain, we follow a broader vision than immediate gratification affords. Indeed, in the short-run, it is often easier to gratify than to abstain, to choose short-term over long-term gains. Such a pleasure principle is a common social and individual standard.

Ironically, sexual abstinence, not sexual indulgence, is countercultural. In the sixties, the free expression of sexual behavior was countercultural, but now the free expression of sexual abstinence has become countercultural. Abstinence is not the cultural "in" thing to do. To go against the trend, to question common assumptions, and to abstain from satisfaction in service of different values are rarely promoted. It takes courage, inner strength, and a healthy identity to stand up differently in the midst of cultural and peer pressures.

Nevertheless, abstinence is beginning to be offered as another choice, often because it is the only guaranteed method of preventing unwanted consequences. Although various forms of birth control have helped to decrease sexually transmitted diseases and pregnancies, they have been far from completely effective. Indeed, there is no absolute safe sex, but more accurately, there is less dangerous sex. The only exception is abstinence.

Some people criticize abstinence as unrealistic, contending that it is foolish to expect people, especially adolescents and young adults, to abstain. They seem to assume that sex is too strong or people are too weak. Although this can be true, must it be so? Hopefully, we can attain a freedom where sex is not overwhelming, and we can choose to abstain if we have good reasons to do so.

Eighteen-year-old Jason gives some of his reasons. "Just because I'm not sexually active does not mean that I have a problem. I have sexual feelings as much or more than anyone else. And yet, some of my friends think there's something wrong with me. They assume that I must have problems especially since a lot of women are attracted toward me. Even the girls wonder about me. I guess they think I'm gay or something.

"What also gets me angry is the so-called sex education lectures in health class. What a joke. The physiology of sexuality is given, which is okay, but I can read about that. Then they show all the various forms of birth control, giving the pros and cons of each. They also mention abstinence with a controlled snicker, like there's something wrong with it.

"Why don't they spend as much time on abstinence as they do on contraception? Why don't they teach us ways to practice abstinence? They don't spend nearly as much time on abstinence as they do on so-called safe sex. Why not?

"I'm abstinent because I think it's a better way. Not only is it the safest sex, but there are advantages as well. For me abstinence makes life simpler. I'm too busy with studies and athletics to get involved. And, I don't want to be hurt or to hurt a girl. To me, sex is serious; it's not a play thing.

"I want to become educated and successful. Many years of school are ahead of me, and I don't have time to mess around. After med school, I hope I'm ready to be committed and then enjoy sex. Until then, I'll survive as a virgin. Maybe I'll even thrive."

This emerging adult has a good sense of identity and wants to deepen and solidify himself before he enters a sexual relationship. He also has set goals, and he plans to achieve them. Furthermore, he takes sex seriously, being sensitive not only to himself but also to women. It sounds like he takes pride in being a sexual celibate.

Some others mock the notion of abstinence. They say it comes from religious extremists, or is out of touch with the real world, and therefore is not to be taken seriously. Indeed, in some instances their criticisms may be valid insofar as some religious approaches lack clinical credibility and efficacy. Nevertheless, this does not have to be and often is not the case. Although abstinence can be a sign of denial, rationalization, or repression, healthy abstinence is in service of openness, truth, and freedom.

Remember, abstinence is not an exclusion of sexual gratification, but rather an avoidance of stimulation and genital behavior. Abstaining from genital gratification means that we are still genital as well as sexual in a myriad of other ways. We have shown that being a man or a woman, masculine or feminine, affectionate and intimate are forms of sexuality. When practicing sexual abstinence, we are still sexual but not genital in our behavior. Paradoxically, we abstain from sex while being sexual.

Abstinence makes sense not only in preventing disease and pregnancy but also in maintaining and fostering health. So, while the positive consequences of abstinence include the prevention of pregnancy and STD's, there are other important consequences. Consider some of the psychosocial advantages of abstinence.

Psychosocial Consequences

Abstinence involves a discipline—a willingness and ability to say no to immediate gratification in service of long-term gains. Refraining from genital gratification while gratifying other sexual modes can be a strengthening exercise that relies on and engenders control and confidence. Rather than being impulse driven, we exercise more freedom. Rather than automatically reacting to genital desires, we expand our spectrum of choices. Rather than our desires being in control, we are in control. Rather than following the mistaken message of mass media, we choose to be true to ourselves. Rather than succumbing to peer pressure, we stand autonomously for health. Choosing to avoid the easier and more pleasant way of genital gratification can strengthen our ego functions and self-esteem.

Freedom to abstain from the benefits of genital gratification presupposes and reinforces self-confidence and self-esteem. "I'm not sure why, but I feel better when I say no to spending a night with a fellow," says Sarah. "I'm not talking about any guy, but a man whom I have known for sometime. Or when I meet a man for the first time, it makes sense not to get physically involved. There is something about setting these limits that makes me feel stronger and freer."

Saying no in service of control, freedom, and well-being strengthens us. Abstinence combats narcissism, our propensity to think too much about ourselves. It ameliorates needs for self-gratification, self-affirmation, and self-actualization that can overtake and diminish us. Refusing to nurture our narcissistic self enables us to be aware of and attentive to the needs and feelings of ourselves and others.

An avoidance of genital involvement can also help us be open to and honest about what is going on within ourselves and with others. We are not as likely to be clouded by the mystique of sex, particularly when a situation is problematic. Genital involvement can cover interpersonal problems, impede open communication, and prevent conflict resolution. Sex rarely resolves anything. Conversely, abstinence can help us to face and talk about issues in service of effective adjustment and resolution. Indeed, research confirms that couples who abstain from pre-marital sex have a higher probability of marital success than couples who do not abstain.

For various reasons, temporary abstinence is appropriate in marriage. Becky, for example, points to the seductive nature of sex. "Look, I love my husband, and he's a pretty good guy and even a better father. I appreciate that. But, when we have a disagreement or when I get upset, he shuts up and withdraws. Later, he buys me a gift, and then wants to have sex. This gets me more mad, and then I feel guilty. Then I give in and have sex.

"When sex is over, Jim is a happy camper. It's as if he feels that everything is all right. I have mixed feelings because we never talked about the issues that upset me. Although the sex felt good, I still feel upset, for nothing was resolved. I'm getting tired of using sex as the cure-all. It doesn't cure anything. Maybe I should stop this charade."

In time, many married women (and some men) abstain from sex as a protest against using sex as an ineffective way to resolve problems. Women (primary sexuality) are more inclined to talk about issues and to achieve some rapport before sex. In this way, abstinence can be in service of greater intimacy. Men (primary sexuality) are more inclined to put difficulties aside and invest their energy in genital sex, falsely assuming that sex well resolve problems. To the contrary, sex should usually be an affirmation and celebration of achieving reconciliation before sex.

Abstinence presupposes and enhances our cognitive clarity and volitional choice. Detaching from sexual passion helps to keep a clear vision, one that is not obscured with genital urgency. The ecstasy of genital behavior can be restrictive in that it obfuscates other worlds of meaning. Being immersed in passion, it is easy to sexualize reality and forget about other feelings. Again, freedom is curtailed, not fostered.

Margaret gives her reasons for abstinence. "Most Friday nights we go out to party, and I'll slip and have sex. I'm always stoned when I get involved. And it's never really good. When I stay sober, I'm better off, and I have more fun. And most importantly, I don't have to deal with the consequences of letting myself be used. I'm simply in a better place when I don't get sucked into sexual games.

"So I have to be careful not to get caught up in the whirlwind of sex and drugs. It's a lethal combination. Even without drugs, sex is hypnotic. To me, it's a drug. It dulls my senses and I don't think and act in my best interests. To me, that's a drug.

"True, I drift off into a different world, and it can be interesting and exciting. But, I also take risks; not just STD's but also my reputation can be on the line. Maybe more importantly, I'm vulnerable. Who knows what kind of nut a guy may turn out to be. I could get hurt. Clearly, it's better for me to abstain from drugs and sex."

Instead of being mutually exclusive, abstinence and freedom are interrelated. The freedom of expression, the freedom of choice, the freedom from negativity, and the freedom for health demands discipline and abstinence. Free and healthy people abstain. To keep physically fit, it is necessary to diet—to abstain from certain kinds and amounts of foods. To be psychologically healthy, it is necessary to abstain from unhealthy behavior. To relate well interpersonally, it is necessary to maintain appropriate boundaries while communicating with care. To grow spiritually, it is necessary to abstain from impediments to spiritual growth.

Although successful people are not always healthy, success does demand abstinence. To use one's time, energy, and space efficiently involves abstinence. For instance, to succeed in athletics or music involves considerable discipline to set limits and practice as well as to abstain from indulgence that shortens and often ruins one's career. To succeed in practically anything of value usually means rigorous and long hours, which automatically include abstaining from other activities.

Abstinence also helps us to assess and avoid situations that we would later regret. Knowing that abstinence is a viable and valid choice, we are less likely to be manipulated or to manipulate. Remember: Sexuality implies a spiritual promise of care. So, when we are hurt in a sexual relationship, it is our soul that suffers most. Abstinence enables us to set appropriate boundaries in order to protect and take care of our bodies/spirits.

Spiritual Consequences

It is hardly a quirk that religions encourage abstinence outside a marital context. Increasingly more studies show that spiritual people are apt to live longer and better than those who are not spiritual. Vowed religious women are prime examples. Spiritual people learn the art of fasting in services of feasting. For Buddhist monks and Christian religious, celibacy is not a declaration of the evil of sex, but rather a proclamation of its transcendent dimension. These people vow celibacy for the sake of the Kingdom not after death but on earth. Their vowed life, including chaste celibacy, heralds our primary and ultimate reason for being: to live freely in peace, to grow older together in Love.

We have emphasized the transcendent movement of spirituality to go beyond ourselves, to "the more than." The powerful beauty of sexuality is that it is spiritual as well as embodied, sensuous, and erotic. The paradox is that we humans strive for the unlimited in limited ways, and sexuality is one of the best demonstrations of this dynamic process. In genital excitement, we—our genitals and other sexual parts—try to go beyond our individual selves and desire connection. We go out not only to other people but also to a Greater Power/Care, to Buddha, Confucius, Mohammed, Jesus, Yahweh, and God. In sex, and especially genital sex, our spirit is moved to seek union, to perfect ourselves by going beyond ourselves.

When we bond with a greater reality than ourselves, we become empowered to see and act wisely.

Indeed, appropriate and healthy sexual behavior maintains and promotes this transcendent movement. Unfortunately, the spirituality of genitality is often forgotten, repressed, bifurcated, or violated. Rather than forgetting the transcendence of genitality, healthy abstinence keeps us aware of this sexual sacredness. Abstinence can preserve, nurture, and proclaim the spirituality of genitality. While being sexually aroused, spiritual awareness can help us to avoid manipulation and exploitation. Appreciating how we are interconnected can motivate us to relate with respectful love. Abstinence pressures us to look for and respond to the Transcendent.

If we are spiritually mindful in sex, we are apt to be respectful of ourselves and others. While combating exploitation and abuse, we are more likely to respond to others as brothers and sisters. Since spirituality moves toward unity and community, we see others as integral parts of the same reality of which we are a member. Such a vision increases the likelihood of free and healthy approaches toward sex.

Mario exemplifies a pragmatically spiritual approach toward spirituality. "I met this beautiful woman at a wedding, and for reasons only God knows, she really came on to me. Maybe it was the wedding spirits operating when she unequivocally told me that she would love to spend the night with me.

"Believe me, this woman had an incredible body. And she was turned on by my body—and I think, by me too. I was very attracted to her. Hum, what to do. Well, let me make a short story shorter.

"I didn't want to come off as some kind of religious nut or holy roller. Actually, I wanted to jump in bed with her forever. My body was intensely turned on. I could easily visualize us making love. Yet, unfortunately or fortunately, I also had these values. And there was a part of me that wanted to get rid of them.

"Well, I told her that I was really attracted to her, that I would love to make lover to her for at least an eternity. But, but, but also, I had these values that I hold sacred, and I can't figure out how to have my cake and eat it too. And she wondered why I couldn't, or at least put my values aside for a while. I chuckled and said that I really wish I could, but to be true to myself (and her), I couldn't.

"When I shared my experience with some of the guys, they said I was crazy to pass up such an opportunity. They looked at me as if I was off my rocker. Yet, I think they were also a bit intrigued with my approach. Thinking back, I'm glad, with some ambivalence, I did what I did. I savored and responded to this woman's incredible sexuality while affirming and respecting her soul."

Mario probably gave this woman a different experience. Here is a man who delighted in a woman's sexuality while connecting with her spirit. He did not play games of sexual exploitation or manipulation. In effect, he said yes to her sexuality and spirit. He said no to something good for something better. Mario abstained from sex while satisfying his sexual spirit.

Paramount to our discussion is that healthy abstinence preserves and promotes the spirituality of sexuality while forgoing genital gratification. Indeed, there may be losses that can engender discomfort, but abstinence offers gains that should outweigh the losses. However, tipping the scale toward abstinence is often difficult. Sexual lust in particular is a common and socially reinforced impediment to abstinence—and, to healthy gratification.

LUST

We have seen how genital behavior of whatever kind makes sense and nonsense. Indeed, people can find it difficult to abstain from genital sex in whatever form because it is so meaningful and powerful. Nevertheless, a central thesis is that we are called to abstain from immature and unhealthy sex—or, lustful sex as well as to gratify healthy sex.

Somewhat simplistically stated: To be healthy, we must abstain from lustful sex. But, what is lust? To define it is not easy, for lust has many meanings, ranging from healthy to normal to unhealthy. For instance, a lust for life or a lustful love may indicate an enthusiastic way of living, a *carpe diem et noctem* approach. Such a so-called healthy lust is often a synonym for zestful living and passionate behavior. However, lust refers more frequently to seeing and treating others as sex objects, viewing people primarily in their physical/sexual dimension. At the end of this continuum, lust can be pathological as evidenced in addictive behaviors. Usually, lust has a pejorative meaning in health and recovery programs.

Although lust can be extended to various contexts, it commonly has a sexual connotation. Lust indicates an intense sexual desire or craving. In lust, we sexually crave to possess and consume; we are caught up in our appetite to devour another.

Phil proclaims his lust. "I just love porno movies. And now with the Internet, I'm in my glory. It's such a relief to lose myself in the heat of sex. It's as if my whole world condenses into intense sex. Stress is reduced, and I can get away from everything for a while. I simply lose myself in pleasure. I feel so alive, focused and yet groggy.

"Cybersex is a lot safer and less costly than drugs. And, I have control over the pace and intensity of my excitement. Not so with drugs. It's just a very accessible and easy escape into a place where I am in control and where I can be anonymous.

"Sure, virtual reality is not as good as the real thing, but in some respects it's better. As I said, I'm not as vulnerable and I can orchestrate and direct this symphony of sex. Unlike a real woman, these women are always there for me. I suppose that they are a bit sexist and certainly ageist. But who would want to have sex with an old person? Serve me young stuff."

Besides other issues, Phil voices an interesting thought, namely: Why are old people less likely to be objects of lust? Even in mass media, the elderly are rarely portrayed as lust objects, and when they are, these elderly try to act and look young. There are probably many reasons for this phenomenon, and few if any are healthy. Actually these reasons can give us insight into the nature and activity of lust as well as help us abstain.

Objects of lust predominantly fall into the first half of the life span. People over fifty, particularly women, are not seen with lascivious eyes nearly as often as young women. Why? Perhaps our criteria for attraction, like smooth skin, less fat and more muscle tone, quicker movements, more hormonal communications, and greater physicality fit "not old" people. Perhaps younger people genitalize sex and thereby follow a male model. Perhaps lustful people are younger not only chronologically but also psychosocially and spiritually.

Perhaps old people are rarely objects of lust not only because of how they look physically and behave socially and psychologically, but also because of their spiritual selves. Being closer to death, the elderly are apt to manifest spirit, which militates against lust. It is reasonable to contend that there is an inverse relation between lust and spirit. The more spirit there is, the less lust there is.

In light of our wholistic paradigm, lust is understood as despiritualized sex. In lust, we repress, minimize, or forget the spirit of sex, and at our worst we try to dissociate sex from its spirit. Consequently, the centripetal force of sex engenders and fosters an orientation of taking, using, and narcissistic self-absorption. When our physical self takes over, tension increases with a simultaneous demand for relief. Consequently, we are apt to experience people as objects and functions for our gratification.

The spirit, never completely expunged, is manipulated in the direction of self-gratification. Actually, lust violates the spirit as much as or more than the body. It makes sense, for instance, that people who are the objects of lust feel resentment, for their dignity and integrity are violated. Or think of an extreme form of lust: pedophilia. What upsets most people as much or more than physical exploitation is the power that is employed to seduce, manipulate, and abuse a child. People intensely feel a child's vulnerability and helplessness and the heinous affront to a child's soul. Indeed, a child's physical wounds heal, but the spiritual wounds may remain forever.

Lust is a futile attempt to displace spirit. In fact, the adumbrated spirit in lust is part of lust's powerful attraction. Lust lures us with counterfeits of spirit like illusions of complimentarity, oneness, and peace, and these gifts are presented in the wrappings of immediate pleasure and easy availability. Unlike a spiritual journey, which includes difficult times, lust entices us with the illusion of instant fulfillment. And since our spirit is minimized, our fulfillment is temporary and fragmented.

Lustful sex makes more nonsense than sense. Lust neither manifests nor fosters health; at best it maintains us. One might ask what is wrong with maintaining oneself. What is not good about it is that our nature seeks more than mere maintenance; our existence seeks to go beyond itself. Furthermore, lust is based on the false belief of individualism—that our primary nature is to be independent and self-sustaining. Lust violates our true nature of radical interdependence.

Since lust offers us the illusion of spiritual interconnectedness, we suffer consequences. Such sex seductively shackles our spirit, virtue is underdeveloped, and character weakens. With spirit, we grow in inner strength, equanimity, and freedom. With lust, we fixate in relative weakness, anxiety, and slavery. In lust, our vision is constricted, our spectrum of meaning is narrowed, and happiness is temporary. Lust diminishes our being. Lust is shameful.

Thus, lust is not healthy as evidenced in its consequences to self and others—to us. In the present moment, the unhealthy effects are hidden behind a veil of pleasure only to be revealed after we are satiated. Although lust may feel good, lust is lacking; it fails to lead us to a healthy life. Lust falls short of what and who we can and should be. In the next chapter, we will look at how lust is practiced in less than healthy sex.

CHAPTER NINE
LESS THAN HEALTHY SEX

I have discussed how marriage is the situation that can afford the proper time, place, and commitment for healthy and good genital sex. Although the state of marriage does not guarantee healthy genital sex, other situations do not offer this opportunity.

Also, I described how genital sex calls for love. The sacred and sensual experiences of genital love demands wholeness and holiness if it is to bear fruit in healthy and spiritual living. Genital sex is healthy when those who share it are affirmed, appreciated, and enjoyed as whole persons. Nevertheless, genital sex can fall short of this intention.

When we fail to look with eyes of love, we are apt to forget the spiritual in sexuality, making it easier and more tempting to engage in sex that is less than the healthy ideal. In this chapter, we will consider less than healthy sexual behaviors, why and how they are attractive, and when, why, and how it is better to abstain.

People's views and responses to sexual behavior like masturbation, homosexuality, and pornography have changed over the past fifty years. Presently, many people feel little or no compunction about them, but this was not always the case. Nonmarital genital gratification evoked more guilt than hostility and injustice, and was felt to be a one-way ticket to hell. Sexuality, in general, was treated as an "enemy" or only as a means for procreation rather than a gift and opportunity for pleasure as well as spiritual and psychological growth.

Because of such negative assessments of sexuality, denial and repression of sexual feelings were common. Others escaped self-awareness by overindulgence (eating, drinking, working), irritable behavior (towards authorities, peers, or subjects), or acting out sexually (with others or self in fantasy or reality). As we have seen, however, such negative coping increases tension rather than purges it, resulting in frustration and anxiety as well as acting-out.

The "new way" fosters free expression and guiltlessness. In mass media models, sexual satisfaction is assumed to be a right, and to abstain is unrealistic, stupid, or a symptom of repression. Seldom is sexual abstinence portrayed as a viable option that is healthier than satisfaction. Satisfying "my own" needs, insisting that "my body is mine," "having" good feelings or "not hurting others" are conventional justifications for sexual gratification. Since discomfort is often assumed to indicate something wrong, the practices of suppression, mortification, and sublimation are judged masochistic, old-fashioned, or simply naïve and unrealistic.

NONMARITAL HETEROSEXUALITY

Nonmarital sex has become an accepted and frequently promoted practice. We have seen that it can be attractive and seductive, especially to those who feel empty and lonely. Such persons are particularly vulnerable to genital involvement since sex can numb pain and gives the illusion of fulfillment. Emptiness quickly returns, however, often more intensely.

Here are one woman's reflections about such a situation. "Sometimes almost anybody would seem better than nobody. When I feel so lonely, I wish someone would just hold and hug me. I yearn to be touched and cherished, to know that I am worthy of being loved. Sex isn't really what I'm after, but I know it usually comes with male affection. And I have to admit that sex brings excitement and intimacy to my boring and lonely life. Yet, as time goes on it doesn't really work out. Nothing seems to last. Invariably I end up where I started, yearning for connection. I feel that sex doesn't really give me what I want and need. Yet, it's better than nothing. Or is it? Something very important is missing."

This woman manifests one type of nonmarital sexual involvement. Her loneliness seeks love, and she is willing to get sexually involved for affection. Although she enjoys the sexual relationship, love is more important. So far, she has found that most men choose temporary gratification, while she longs for an endearing and enduring relationship.

Indeed, nonmarital sex can be considered on a broad continuum that varies from the most crass and unhealthy to the most tender and intimate. For instance, recreational sex between strangers differs considerably from sex between an engaged couple. In the former situation, the partners are likely to using each other for fleeting pleasure. Committed lovers come close to the optimum conditions of marriage.

Consider, for example, an engaged couple that genuinely love each other and understandably move towards genital love. With honest and good intentions, they desire to express their love through sexual intercourse. Sexual behavior would affirm their love, and yet their sexual relationship would not quite be what it is meant to be. Such a statement may sound moralistic or unrealistic, but clinical and empirical data gives support for such a position. On the one hand, sex would be a celebration and strengthening of their love. On the other hand, the relative lack of appropriate time and space would cause stress that could erode their love. Indeed, engaged couples that practice pre-marital sex are more likely to divorce. Abstinence is a better way.

Consider sexual love between friends. Genital sex can express love while it lessens tension and increases self-esteem; moreover, such friends probably and understandably dislike abstinence, yet their love will eventually be challenged and may even begin to dissipate. Such a consequence occurs because healthy genital sex calls for marital time, place, and commitment, and friendship does not afford these conditions. Sex between friends calls for a new relationship, namely marriage, or it threatens to destroy the friendship. Friendship also calls for abstinence.

An argument can be made that two unmarried persons living together do have the time, place, and perhaps commitment to have healthy sex. Indeed, this kind of relationship is meaningful, but it usually lacks the permanent commitment that genital behavior demands for on-going growth. Although the situation is more convenient than persons not living together, the appropriate commitment is lacking. Abstaining from such a relationship is difficult, for cohabitation is popular and meaningful. Listen to this woman.

"I really care for Jim, and I think he really cares for me. And we get along pretty well. Besides, sharing the same apartment saves money and is convenient. But I wonder if we will ever get married, or if I even want to. What really makes me uneasy is that I know he can walk out at any time. For that matter, so can I. We seldom talk about it.

"In some ways I feel like I'm always walking on eggshells, like I have to be too good. It's as if there isn't any room for argument or even disagreements. I always have to be at my best. It's like playing house. And when we do have our inevitable difficulties, we have sex, as if sex makes everything all right. Sure, sex does feel good and brings us closer, but our issues are not faced and resolved. Instead of talking, we have sex. Sex is almost like a drug: We have sex when life is difficult. It's confusing. Somehow it's not really real."

A common assumption is that living together is a good preparation for a successful marriage. As we have already stated, studies indicates that people who co-habitat are significantly less likely to succeed in marriage than people who do not co-habitat. Sexual behavior may give the illusion of problem solving and growth but actually it avoids and even exacerbates issues. Pre-marital co-habitation does not give assurance of permanence to a potential marriage; the opposite is more likely.

Recreational sex is also common, but it, too, is not to be recommended. o reaffirm, when we fail to treat one another as whole persons, we impede the spiritual dynamic of connectedness, and consequently feel disconnected and incomplete. Although we physically connect, our unity quickly dissipates, and we can become even more frustrated. Our fulfillment is temporary and fails to foster healthy growth.

Perhaps more subtly, such sex can occur in marriage as well. For instance, partners who consistently have sex only to satisfy physical needs do not enjoy good and healthy sex. A typical example of this is the husband who has a quick orgasm, using his wife as a sperm receptacle, and then falls asleep without regard for his wife. The woman experiences little enjoyment and probably feels used and abused. Indeed, a woman can be just as exploitive and selfish. Surely, such fast sex can be appropriate as a change of pace and can be congruent with a healthy marriage. But as a frequent or exclusive practice it does not allow for the time and space that is needed to express love. Having sex is expedient; making love takes time. Having sex without making love engenders regressive narcissism and disharmony rather than promoting progressive unity and peace.

My contention is that single or celibate lovers have the opportunity to perfect all modes of intimacy except the genital and those that foster or lead to it. In contrast to married people who focus primarily on each other, single persons can be relatively more open to others. Indeed, celibates can be intimate with a particular person, but their intimacy need not take a marital form. And to be sure, single lovers are sexual in that they are affectionate men and women. Thus, it is accurate to say that they are sexual celibates.

MASTURBATION

Many health specialists consider sexual gratification, with self or another, to be a sensible source of pleasure and a healthy practice. Abstinence is inferior to gratification, and at worst unhealthy. Since masturbation is commonly accepted and often recommended, it may behoove us to look closely at its practice and dynamics. This analysis can also help us understand and cope with other sexual behaviors as well.

In the "old days" (not very long ago), many people were taught that masturbation was one of the worst sins. It was suggested that masturbation was a cause of mental and physical illness; even that surgical intervention could be a treatment for masturbation. In those days, it was common to overemphasize sexual sins. When masturbation (acting out) was the coping mechanism for repressed or non-integrated sexuality, a circular and frustrating causality would emerge: masturbation relieves tension, followed by guilt, followed by tension, which led again to masturbation, and so on and on. Many health specialists now consider masturbation to be a convenient tension reducer and a productive way to realize body awareness and potential – in general, a healthy practice.

From my wholistic perspective, I personally support neither the new nor the old positions; I contend that masturbation is seldom unhealthy in and of itself. Unlike many professionals, however, I do not think that masturbation should be recommended. Psychologically, masturbation is not a one-way ticket to hell, nor to heaven. Masturbation is an earthly matter, neither healthy nor unhealthy. It is a conventional way of reducing tension, evoking pleasure, and acquiring a degree of normal maintenance.

Sociologically, masturbation is "normal" in that most people at some time in their lives more or less practice it. It falls within the parameter of "normal" or acceptable behavior. Psychologically, masturbation can be considered normal because it temporarily reduces tension and makes life immediately easier (though not better) as well as helps one to cope in the short run. Nevertheless, although masturbation can be considered in this sense normal, I contend that it is not healthy because it impedes spiritual growth.

Dynamics

To understand the dynamics of masturbation, it is important to look at the life of one who masturbates in light of a total process. One element of this context is age. For example, adolescents usually feel more strongly than children and adults the urgency and confusion of new genital desires. Also, they experience peer and cultural pressure to satisfy them. An adult who has repressed his or her genital feelings may masturbate for reasons like those of an adolescent: urgency, novelty, pleasure, curiosity, and environmental pressure.

Frequency and intensity are also important factors. Masturbation once a month differs from doing it once a day in terms of psychosocial and spiritual impact. Compulsive masturbation involves a significant part of one's life. In contrast, some people generally abstain from masturbation but periodically "act out" for a relatively short time. Others follow a cyclic patter: They allow tension to build up, periodically relieve it, and then wait for it to increase again.

Here's one adolescent's reflection on masturbation. "I'm not real guilty about it, but I'm not proud of it. Most of the guys do it at some time or another. I think there are some guys who don't, so I guess it can be done. I masturbate when I'm especially horny, or when I'm bored and have a lot of time. It relieves the tension, but I have to admit that the tension always returns. Masturbation doesn't seem to get you anywhere."

Intensity of involvement is significant. The amount of time as well as the quantity and quality of self-investment affect the impact masturbation has on one's life. Someone who masturbates daily with intense fantasy as the primary source of intimacy will differ significantly from a person who masturbates infrequently and who has healthy experiences of intimacy.

Masturbation is particularly seductive because it is an easy and accessible way to reduce tension and to explore genital feelings and fantasies without interpersonal vulnerability, responsibility, or accountability. It seems one has license to masturbate almost whenever he or she feels like it. One need not worry about other people or social consequences; it can be kept to oneself.

Part of masturbation's lure is the safe secrecy of fantasy: One does not have to risk rejection or failure. It gives the illusion of being invulnerable, open, and perfect. Instead of engaging in real relationships, the individual can create a world of make-believe people where anything is possible and there are no limits.

A subtle attraction of masturbation is that the initial choice often emerges from non-genital experiences; for instance, boredom, anxiety, and especially loneliness may urge us to masturbate. Masturbation numbs the discomfort of emptiness and incompleteness and promises some semblance of being one with self. But these rewards are short-lived. The frustrating irony is that the escape from loneliness actually impedes the attainment of the true goal of genitality: interpersonal intimacy.

Sense and Nonsense

Like any sexual act, masturbation involves a yearning for intimacy and completeness. This transcendent dynamic is evident when the body visibly moves out for more than oneself. Its hidden meaning is that we are being moved to go beyond ourselves to another, to more than self-containment.

The folly of masturbation (as well as recreational sex) is that it silences the urge to love. Masturbation turns the self inward, while impeding the true longing for intimacy with another. The transcendent force in sex returns to oneself aborting, an opportunity for growth and engendering emptiness and loneliness.

A particular danger of frequent masturbation is narcissism: pleasurable self-preoccupation. Someone who masturbates habitually is inclined toward immediate gratification and to seeing others in terms of self-satisfaction. A married person who masturbates or has masturbated frequently and intensely may unconsciously use his or her spouse for self-satisfaction. This individual is conditioned to assume that he has the right to sexual satisfaction when he wants it. Not to be satisfied is felt as unjust or wrong. Even though this selfish motive may be unconscious, it nevertheless impedes intimacy, for the focus is on "me", not us.

Masturbation is superficial, maximizing the physical and minimizing the spiritual. Sexual gratification without spiritual involvement is surface contact that can lead to shallow living. Minimizing the spirit in sex eventually leads to more frustration, for what we seek – union, completion, and ongoing growth – eludes us. It affirms the absence of real presence. It is no wonder why masturbation in spite of its acceptance is seldom a source of pride.

Here are the comments of a man who recognizes his folly: "It's not easy to talk about it. It is easier to brag about having sex with women. It's embarrassing. Masturbation is a habit with me and I wish I could stop it. I try and try, and I fail and fail. Sometimes I can go for weeks without doing it, but it always returns. It's like an addiction. To compound matters, I can't seem to stop logging onto the Internet; you know: cybersex. It's so easy, so available, so safe. And, there is so much to see and fantasize about. I try to stop, but I just keep going back to it. I guess virtual sex is safe and easy. Maybe masturbation is a substitute for real intimacy. Still, it's no fun being lonely."

In short, masturbation falls short of the nature of healthy sex. It does not lead to and celebrate union with another or on-going growth. It does, however, give the fleeting illusion of these and other spiritual consequences. The meaning of masturbation can vary from mere maintenance to a challenging obstacle to problematic narcissism. At best, masturbation impedes the spirituality of sexuality, and at worst the spiritual is violated.

HOMOSEXUALITY

Homosexuality remains a controversial as well as a debated and unsettling issue. Some people think homosexuality is a perversion, a disease, a sin, or at best not good. Homophobes may avoid, criticize, or attack homosexuals, while some homophiles treat homosexuals better than heterosexuals. Others contend that homosexuals, while maintaining a different sexual preference, can function as well as heterosexuals and should be treated equally. Some feel that homosexuality is a better orientation. Many are not sure and wonder about homosexuality.

Before pronouncing judgment on homosexuality, it is wise to question yourself. What do I think? What is homosexuality? Who or what is a homosexual? How do I feel about homosexuality? How do I truly treat homosexuals? Do I really understand the world of homosexuals? Do I say one thing, but do another? What do I really believe? More importantly, how do I interact with homosexuals?

Instead of categorizing homosexuals, it is better to speak of "homosexualities" and homosexuals rather than homosexuality. Furthermore, to identify persons with a part of them, in this case their sexuality, is unjust and harmful. Homosexuals differ as much as heterosexuals. For instance, most homosexuals are not effeminate, and effeminate men are not necessarily homosexuals. All interior decorators and hairdressers are not gay, and not all athletes and truck drivers are straight. Like their heterosexual brethren, some homosexuals are unhealthy and need help, while others are normal in that they cope, succeed, and look and act as most people do. Still others are healthy.

How many homosexuals are there in the population? Nobody knows for sure. Much depends on one's definition of homosexuality. One estimate is between 2 and 10% of the population. Whatever the percentage, homosexuality is not the norm. And since it is not the norm, it is more unsettling and studied.

In our context, homosexuality is construed as the condition of experiencing an erotic preference for members of one's own sex. Homosexual men can and frequently are attracted to women but not erotically just as heterosexual men can be attracted to other men. However, someone who frequently yearns for and fantasizes about genital relations exclusively with one's own sex is probably homosexual.

Homosexuals often demonstrate greater sensitivity toward women than heterosexual men. Not surprisingly, many women feel more comfortable with homosexual men because they can be intimate with them without being concerned about genital arousal or involvement. As we have seen, genital involvement carries with it complications, responsibilities, and consequences. Without the complexity of genital involvement, homosexual men and women often feel freer together. That is, in some respects, women may be more intimate and freer with homosexual men than with heterosexual men.

It is important to realize people do not choose their sexual orientation. Just as heterosexuals do not decide to be "straight," homosexuals do not choose to be "gay." Rather, they find themselves to be "gay." So if we do not choose our orientation, what causes our sexual orientation?

Theories

Like most studies, there are three broad approaches that focus on nature, nurture, or a combination of both. Some scientists believe that homosexuality has a hereditary and genetic basis. Others propose hormones or neurological factors. Still others conjecture that during a critical period of childhood a preferred sex can become firmly entrenched. The emotionally distant or unavailable father is a popular theory in the environmental camp. And many professionals see homosexuality as both a matter of inheritance and learning; they propose that people are born with a predisposition of homosexuality, which is then nurtured in the environment. The bottom line is that we really do not conclusively know what causes homosexuality, or for that matter, heterosexuality.

Theories of and research on female homosexuality are even less developed and valid. One common but far from conclusive hypothesis in the nurture camp is that homosexual women come from dysfunctional families consisting of a cruel father and martyred mother The theory adds that lesbians frequently have traits related to dominance, status seeking, intellectual efficiency, and endurance. According to this theory, a homosexual woman tends to be strong partly to prevent men from causing the chaos suffered when the woman was a child. Again, this theory and others are attempts to explain a lesbian orientation; they are neither proven nor unproven.

Research does show some interesting differences between male and female homosexuals. For instance, a lesbian is more likely to have longer lasting feelings of attachment to one partner. Male relationships, on the other hand, are usually short-loved and throughout a lifespan usually include many partners. Also, some studies indicate that about two thirds of declared lesbians are bisexuals in that they have had or will have heterosexual experiences. In light of our wholistic approach, let us look at the world of homosexuals.

It is important to appreciate the non-homogenital motivations in the lives of homosexuals. For instance, some homosexuals feel compelled to visit homosexual places by a sense of adventure that brings excitement and risk. Others seek out other homosexuals in order to "be with"—to find acceptance as a member of a community and to escape the alienation of being labeled "one of them." Some homosexuals, especially when bored and lonely, desire a setting where they can be themselves without pretense. Many homosexuals experience a special at-homeness, acceptance, and understanding as well as freedom in homosexual situations.

Some homosexuals feel as if they live in two worlds: the straight world and the gay world. This dual life can become exhausting. Finding a time and place for homosexual involvement becomes a tedious task. Not infrequently, stress pressures a person to come out of his closet and pursue the gay life more openly or to be celibate.

Homosexuals should be judged and treated with the same justice and charity that heterosexuals should get. There is no need for double standards. Heterosexuals should not view homosexuals as lower than themselves —and, homosexuals should not see heterosexuals as lower than they. Especially from a spiritual perspective, we are all interconnected parts of the same whole, members of the same body. To give or expect different treatment because of one's orientation seems to be contrary to spiritual dynamics.

It is only fair to use the same standards for homosexual as for heterosexual involvement. Unfortunately, many people use questionable double standards. I do not condone homogenital relations just as I do not condone heterogenital relations outside of a healthy marital relationship. Abstinence or chaste celibacy is the preferred way. Thus, genital sex is restricted, while primary and affective sex is promoted.

Like heterosexuals, homosexuals can be just as healthy, immature, normally mad, or unhealthy as heterosexuals. Although homosexuals vary just as much as heterosexuals, research concludes that homosexual men manifest relatively more mental health problems than heterosexual men and women. The cause of this difference is not definitely known, but social rejection and oppression are etiological hypotheses.

Some people contend that a homosexual relationship can be healthy when it fosters growth. These people make a distinction between unhealthy promiscuous homosexuality and healthy homosexuality accompanied by care and fidelity. They argue that homosexual marriages do exist. In fact, little empirical data exist to support existence of such permanent relationships. For the few who do live together for a long time, the relationship is more aptly described as a celibate friendship. Or, a homosexual couple may live together with functional and emotional commitment but without the fidelity that genital relations call for. As in heterosexual marriages, this unfaithfulness cannot be condoned. Research suggests that long term homosexual relationships exist, though rarely; however, when such relationships do exist, they lack sexual fidelity. Thus, genital experiences between persons of the same gender lack the constant fidelity that healthy marriages demand.

From out spiritual-sexual perspective, it can be argued that in a homogenital relationship the transcendent dimension of genital love is aborted. Unlike heterogenital relations, homogenital relations neither go beyond themselves nor can they be procreative—a sacred sign of transcendence.

My positions are that homosexual behavior should be accepted and promoted in its primary and affective forms, but in its genital dimension, abstinence is appropriate. Homogenital intimacy does not promote the progressive and transcendent growth that is possible in marital heterogenital relationships. To be sure, primary and affective homosexuality can promote ongoing growth. And of course, all heterosexual relationships do not promote integral and ongoing growth. In short, many homosexuals can be and are healthy, but homogenital intimacy is incongruent with our wholistic model.

If this approach is valid, homosexuals are called to be celibate. Such celibate lovers can love and function well with both sexes, though differently. They may have homosexual feelings and fantasies, while abstaining from homogenital relations. Although this can be painfully difficult at times, their sexual desires can challenge and motivate them to grow in chaste abstinence.

This approach can seem and may be unfair, particularly to a homosexual person. Homosexuals are challenged, as many unmarried heterosexuals are, to control and integrate their genital desires without gratifying them. Perhaps homosexuals must be stronger and healthier than their heterosexual brothers and sisters.

Consider the feelings of this forty-five year old man: "In adolescence I noticed that I was different than most others. I simply did not care to be intimate with girls, but I did desire it with guys. This confused and scared me. It was a heavy and lonely burden to carry. And I felt sad and angry when my friends would joke about gays—queers and fagots they called them. Although I have had some homosexual experiences since then, I have usually been celibate. Sometimes it is very difficult. It seems unfair. I didn't choose to be gay, but that's what I am and I accept it. I know I'm not sick because I'm gay; I'm just as healthy as anyone else. But I feel that many people judge me as sick, sinful, or abnormal."

Pseudo Homosexualities, Homophobias, and Friendships

Homosexuality as a constant orientation differs from transitory, situational, or pseudo homosexualities—homogenital relationships that are relatively short term and often emerge in homosocial situations or where the other sex is unavailable. Persons who have had homogenital experiences once or several times in their life might not be homosexual. Likewise, a heterosexual man who has had a few intimate affairs with women may not necessarily be heterosexual. In short, a few genital experiences do not constitute a sexual orientation.

Here are comments of a man who suffered from unfortunate and unnecessary confusion and guilt: "I've always felt uneasy and guilty about what happened sixteen years ago when my friend and I got sexually involved over a period of seven months. We got very close and shared a lot, and on a couple occasions we masturbated each other. It drove me nuts to think that I might be gay. It was a weight I've carried within me. I was scared to talk to anyone about it. Now I don't feel so weird anymore."

This person may not be homosexual, but if he is, he can learn to deal with it. Although he had some homogenital experiences, he also has desires for and fantasies about women, a symptom of being heterosexual. He may have diagnosed himself falsely. Such pseudo-homosexuality is not rare, especially when a heterosexual relationship is difficult to attain. Actually, such homosexual experiences are not rare in homosocial situations like prisons, the armed services, and seminaries.

Transitory or situational homosexuality may occur between friends who are very sensitive but who have repressed their feelings. For example, Don, who comes from a good but puritanical family and has learned to restrict affective expression, feels called to priesthood. After being in the seminary for a while, he finds himself becoming involved with Mike, a friend who comfortably expresses feelings. The men resonate with and care for each other and become so emotionally involved that they fall into physical expressions of their love. Instead of identifying themselves as homosexuals, Don and Mike can pause and learn from their relationship. People should refrain from categorizing them as impure, evil, or gay, and evaluate their relationship in light of solid psychological and spiritual principles. The two men should get help from a competent professional who understands and appreciates the sense and nonsense of homosocial affection and intimacy. Whether homosexual or heterosexual, Don and Mike should refrain from genital behavior.

Consider the case of Joan and Lisa. Both of them are bright but shy women who decide to attend a women's college. Up until the time they became close friends, neither of them experienced a trusting and affirmative relationship. In the initial phases of their friendship, they feel that everything is possible and nothing impossible: They want to be intimate in every way, including genital, and though they experience some guilt, they are also ecstatic. Furthermore, there is a lesbian group that seems to validate and celebrate their relationship. In the joy of their romantic love, both women feel more alive than ever before. But their heavenly state will eventually end. After divinizing each other, they are likely to experience a "negative" stage where they will begin to focus on each other's limits and imperfections. Consequently, they will be more vulnerable to hurt, bitterness, resentment, and jealousy. If they are willing, however, they can develop an integral friendship that incorporates both their divine and demonic dimensions.

Joan and Lisa can learn to set limits on their expressions of affection.

These women are not necessarily lesbians, although they may be. In any case, they are loving women who originally repressed themselves affectively, then became too physically involved. Although their homogenital experiences should not be condoned, neither should these women be condemned.

Keep in mind that every deep friendship is special and intimate. Friends see each other unlike anyone else see them; they have and are something special. Moreover, the best of friendships are exclusive in that they do exclude others in some ways. Friends understand each other in ways no one else can understand them. Exclusivity in friendship, however, should eventually help friends become more inclusive—more sensitive and compassionate with others. Thus, their initial exclusivity should eventually lead to inclusivity. Friendship should liberate rather than shackle. Genital behavior between friends is not healthy for either heterosexuals or homosexuals, for it eventually destroys the friendship. Although a friendship can be very intimate, it does not include the kind of commitment, time, and space needed for healthy genital love.

Homosocial intimacy—the way a person relates to the same sex socially and affectively—is often more problematic to men than to women. Such homophobia occurs partly because our society makes it difficult for men to be close to one another. If one is male, anything more than a handshake is often ridiculed or seen as a perversion in some cultures and ethnic groups. Personally and culturally, women are freer and more comfortable in the homosocial realm. They are less homophobic. They have learned to be more adept interpersonally with both men and women.

Unlike women, men have difficulty enjoying affection as an end in itself and feel that affection will lead to genital involvement. Thus, many men avoid intimacy with other men because they are afraid that it will lead to genital involvement and therefore be homosexual. Homophobia may be a way of avoiding homosocial intimacy because of fear of homogenital intimacy. Indeed, homophobic people may be latently homosexual, or they may be heterosexual and afraid of homosocial intimacy.

Responding to Homosexuals

How to respond to homosexuals can be particularly important when you are in a situation where there is a high percentage of homosexuals, like some seminaries, novitiates, or artistic subcultures. A starting point is to differentiate between homosexuals as persons and their homosexual acts. Instead of identifying homosexuals with their sexual acts—a judgement that is neither just nor helpful, we can seek to understand them in light of their entire lives. Of course, this approach is true of any person, of any orientation, and with any behavior. Ascertain what homosexual experiences mean to the involved persons and how and in what circumstances did they occur.

Another guideline in understanding homosexual activities is to determine if heterophobia, fear of heterosexual involvement, is present. By focusing on the same sex, some people seek to escape their fear of the opposite sex. A man who focuses exclusively on men may be escaping his fear of women. When confronted with women, such a man may become withdrawn, condescending, or scared. Consequently, he may be vulnerable to homosexual intimacy as a way of being intimate and of avoiding heterosexual intimacy. A woman, too, may desire intimacy with a woman because she never learned to be intimate with men. Perhaps her past experiences were traumatic like having been abused or rejected by men. Quasi-homosexual experiences are likely to be a cover for other problems.

To help others, we start by questioning ourselves. How comfortable am I with my own sexuality? How do I deal with my sexuality? How do we deal with the other sex? How do I feel about homosexuals? Do I manifest what I want to see in others? Do I recognize and behave according to the principle that homosexuals of whatever type are radically the same as I—persons who are members of the same humankind? Instead of calling homosexuals "them," can I embrace homosexuals as brothers and sisters of the same human family? The most important response is to show loving kindness and share a life of love. Without this basic, pre-verbal presence, other forms of help are ineffective and possibly harmful.

How can we help ourselves? What can you do if someone pressures you to enter a homosexual relationship? Or what do you do if you are sexually attracted to a friend and your feelings scare you? First, it is good to take stock of yourself. What part might you have in the relationship? Do your expressions of affection unintentionally elicit different feelings in your friend? Are you unconsciously seeking or wondering what it would be like to engage in homosexual love? Are your conscious intentions (thoughts) the same as your unconscious intentions (feelings)? Can you understand the sense and nonsense of homosexuality? Can you foster chaste love for all people, including homosexuals, and thereby foster healthy relationships?

What can and should we do if we are involved in a homosexual relationship? First of all, we should stop. The same is true for a heterosexual relationship. Stopping calls for discipline, which includes suppression. Another help is to anticipate and sublimate one's feelings and to seek to integrate sexuality and spiritually. As always, the challenge is to appreciate the wholeness of self and others so that chaste love is fostered.

You can question yourself about homosexuality. Do you feel a strong desire to be sexually intimate with someone of the same sex? Do you fantasize only about the same sex? Have you been involved in homosexual acts, or are you involved in transitory sexuality that includes friendship? How does genital sex function in your life? Do you live in two worlds: a sexual world and a spiritual one? What are the nongenital motivations for your homogenital behavior? Instead of repressing your spirit, do you acknowledge God's presence in you—especially in your homosexual feelings and acts?

My position is that both single homosexual and heterosexual men and women are called to be sexual in its primary and affective forms and are called to be abstinent in its genital form. Rather than losing spirit, they can integrate their sexuality, particularly their genitality, with love. We are called to live a chaste life of love. Because of social, cultural, and interpersonal prejudice and oppression, homosexuals will probably have more difficulties than heterosexuals. To be judged harshly and to be alienated are difficult. Thus, to be a chaste and celibate lover is a difficult challenge that calls for discipline and sacrifice that go beyond the conventional ways of living. Without a spiritual life, a celibate life makes little or no sense.

PORNOGRAPHY

With the relatively recent advent of cybersex, pornography has proliferated more than ever. Including the exploitation of children and adolescents, pornography is a very lucrative business. In our context, pornography refers to material such as publications, audio and visual tapes, phone calls, movies, pictures, cybersex, magazines, books, any media whose primary purpose is to elicit lust.

Pornography "safely" satisfies one's curiosity and stimulates fantasy. It offers an idea of what can happen behind closed doors, allowing sexual indulgence without risk of interpersonal involvement. Pornographic books, for example, allow users to engage and test themselves with its characters. Unlike some books, they are easy and pleasurable to read. If the reader is immature about sex or has other problems, he or she will find facile relief in drifting off into another world.

Pornography is not healthy; at best, it is immature. Its purpose is to elicit and nurture lust, and when lust is primary, health dissipates and unhealthiness prospers. Pornography exaggerates the physical dimension of sexuality and minimizes the spiritual, attempting to identity a person with genital sex and to make sex a panacea. Pornography encourages one to see people as willing bodies designed exclusively for satisfaction.

Furthermore, pornography is invariably sexist and ageist. It usually follows a male script with its genitalizing sex, orgasmic focus, and relative lack of affective sexuality. And indeed, pornography is ageist. Seldom are the performers elderly or even middle aged. Rather, they are in their teen or younger, twenties, and thirties. Post-menopausal women are rare. Youth is served. No hints of aging are presented; instead, such sex offers the illusion of eternal youth.

A man who watches several pornographic videos in a short time comments; "I feel highly stimulated, intense, and alive when in it, and yet exhausted and sort of drained when finished. Although I have a pleasurable time, I feel empty and shallow afterward. I feel sort of odd, like I was less than I am." Their reaction occurs because pornography stimulates one's surface self, leaving one to feel superficial and empty. Simply stated, pornography insults its participants by treating them as less than they are. To indulge in pornography is to violate oneself, to treat oneself as a sex object. Lacking respect for one's whole self is to diminish our freedom, dignity, and integrity. We deserve and can do better than treating ourselves as objects of lust.

SEXUAL PATHOLOGIES

Pathological sex is no longer the hidden secret that it once was. Besides formal research, education, and treatment, the media has exposed, portrayed, and written about sick sex, particularly offenses against minors. According to the American Psychiatric Diagnostic Manual (1994, p.493), sexual pathologies are characterized by recurrent and intense sexual urges and arousing fantasies involving non-human objects, suffering or humiliation of oneself or one's partner, or minors or non-consenting persons. A sexual disorder is often called a paraphilia, which etymologically refers to *para* (beyond or a deviation) and *philia* (love or attraction). A paraphilia refers to a sexual attraction that deviates from normal standards.

There are many kinds of paraphilic people. For some, sexual acting out is a consistent part of their lives. Some paraphilics act out periodically or when they are under extreme stress, while others abstain for months and years but eventually act out. Some paraphilics never act out on their disorder, but are abstinent and in recovery.

Sexual disorders include many abnormal acts, such as fetishism (being sexually stimulated with objects), frotteurism (inordinate sexual stimulation involving touching and rubbing against a non-consenting person), and pedophilia (sexual fantasies and activities with a minor). Paraphilias also include sexual masochism (receiving sexual behavior or fantasies with inordinate pain), sexual sadism (initiating sexual acts or fantasies that are violent or humiliating), rape (sex with a non-consenting person), transvestic fetishism (behavior involving cross-dressing), voyeurism (observing unsuspecting people who are naked or engaged in sexual activities), and exhibitionism (exposing one's genitals in public), (DSM IV, 1994, pp.522-532). On the other end of this continuum are sexual pathologies that involve a lack of sexual desire such as hypoactive sexual desire (a lack of sexual desire), sexual aversion, and dysfunctional sexual behavior.

A useful way to look at many sexual pathologies is in terms of addiction. Reflect on sex addiction as an obsessive concern about sex and a compulsion to act on lustful desires that produces desired effects as well as negative consequences to self and others. Although acting on one's sexual addiction can make sense in terms of pleasure and power, the negative consequences to self and others outweigh the so-called positive ones.

Members of sexaholics anonymous will state that lust is a key dynamic in being a sex addict. Lust is an inordinate desire to see and treat others as sex objects for sexual gratification. Recovering sexaholics will also tell you that the paramount danger is replacing God or the spiritual life with sexuality, or separating sexuality and spirituality, or lust. When sexuality and spirituality are integrated, it is not a guarantee of abstinence and recovery, but it does increase their likelihood.

Indeed, there are many forms of sex addiction. For instance, distant sex addictions like exhibitionism and voyeurism seldom involve touching the other. Other forms of sex addiction involve consenting adults such as prostitution or promiscuous sex, while others involve minors. And, there are more "normal" addictions such as being addicted to pornography, masturbation, or loveless sex. Actually, the normal modes of addiction are more numerous than the abnormal ones.

Whatever the sex offense, most known sex offenders are men. We usually do not think of women as being sex offenders. And when we read about a female teacher having sex with one of her students, we are apt to feel more uncomfortable than when the predator is a man. Women do offend against sex, but their behavior is usually not as overt and perceived as socially offensive as men's. For instance, a mother who sleeps with her son, parades immodestly in front of her teenage boy, or who wrestles intimately with her eighteen-year-old may be offending sexually. Even overt female sex offenses tend to be morally and legally minimized and treated differently than male offenses.

More violent sex crimes like rape often involve to some degree counterphobia, that is, a person attacks what he really fears—women. From our perspective, taking victims by force is not only a physical offense, but is more deeply a spiritual offense that degrades and insults the integrity and dignity of women. Besides being a sexual offense, rape can also be seen as a strategy to prostrate women, to keep them lower than men so that men have the illusion of being superior. Violent sex offenders are both sex and power driven.

A particularly heinous sex offense is incest. Incest may involve a variety of behaviors, like inappropriate affection, sexual exposure, fondling, masturbation, fellatio, sodomy, or coitus. Indeed, incest causes serious and chronic problems not only because of the sexual activity but more so because of the broken trust, exploitation of parental power, and convoluted affection. Probably no act is more devastating than incest. If the wounds of incest heal, there is always scar tissue.

Another aspect of sex addiction is our societal preoccupation with sex. In fact, one can argue that our society is sexually addicted and that we are immersed in normal and abnormal sex addiction. Sexual abstinence would be difficult in a perfect world, but it is even more difficult in our sexualized world. Because sex offenses against minors (children and adolescents) have been and will be serious issues of public and private concern, let us consider them more closely.

Pedophilia and Ephebophilia

Until recently, pedophilia (sex with pre-pubescent children) and ephebophilia (sex with post-pubescent youth) evoked denial, collusion, anxiety, enabling defensiveness, hostility, and generally inadequate responses. Even when acting with good intentions, we have seen clerical authorities treat sex offenders and their victims ineffectively and sometimes harmfully. Today, more open and helpful approaches, legal, psychological, and spiritual, are being studied and implemented. We have come from a society of denial and enabling in regards to sex offenses to one that is more open and effective. To be sure, progress must continue.

Profiles of perpetrators include all socio-economic groups, races, and professions. And although we might assume that sex offenders are quite different than we are, the opposite is true; most pedophiles and ephebophiles are relatively normal except in their sexuality. They are unlikely to be weird strangers who come from the other side of the tracks, but are likely to be persons like you and me. They are usually not incorrigible criminals, insane, or psychotic. They are more likely to be concerned, productive, and successful citizens as well as known by the victim's family. A pedophile is more likely to be someone similar and close to you rather than different and distant.

Pedophiles are usually attracted to minors not only sexually but also socially. They usually do well working and recreating with children or adolescents, and consequently they are more likely than others to be in a profession or work that gives them access to activities involving minors. This is not suggested that most adults who deal with minors are sex offenders, or that all perpetrators have ready access to minors. Nevertheless, perpetrators seek situations which allow them to spend inordinate time, qualitatively and quantitatively, with minors. Indeed, they seem to enjoy and get more satisfaction from being with minors than being with peers and other adults. Although many can get along with their peers, they feel freer, more at ease, and special when involved with minors. In a sense, they get a certain high from being with minors that they miss with peers.

Most (75%) pedophiles appear to be normal and mild mannered heterosexual men. Although they function normally, their intimacy is disordered. However, some of these offenders, especially in priesthood, are predominantly ephebophiles and homosexual; that is, they desire and get sexually involved with post-pubescent boys. Contrary to some opinions, most homosexuals (and heterosexuals) do not get involved with minors.

Although many pedophiles and ephebophiles feel tender and affectionate toward their victims, they still abuse them. A sexual offense often involves kissing, fondling, and masturbation rather than intercourse or sodomy. Physical force is not common, but another kind of force is used: seduction with affection and power. A typical scenario usually involves social and affectionate involvement before any explicit sexual contact is made. Ephebophiles often become like big brothers or surrogate fathers to potential victims. They show their victims new worlds of recreation, culture, and education to which the victims have not been exposed, and in this sense, they help the potential victim. Ephebophile priests, for example, invariably form a bond of trust with the victim and often with his family. The relationship is far more than sexual, and this is one reason why it is often difficult for the victim to expose the perpetrator and for the family to admit to the signs of inordinate behavior.

Although pedophiles and ephebophiles are usually ashamed, guilty, and confused about their disordered love and sexuality, it is rare that they voluntarily confess to authorities. Invariably, they have to be caught. When caught, some will admit to their deeds, and many will deny until evidence is overwhelming. Then, most drown in shame.

Listen to the comments of this pedophile. "I don't know why I get involved with little girls. I wish I didn't. It tears me apart to know that I do this and that I have to hide this secret burden. Honestly, I really like and try to help girls, but something gets into me and I go overboard. Sometimes I'll be fine for months, then the demon that always lurks in the shadows starts to pressure me. It seems that the more I fight it, the stronger it gets. Sometimes I sort of plan to get sexually involved, and other times it just happens. When it happens, I feel satisfied and complete, yet ashamed and guilty.

"Yes, I use all kinds of ploys to protect myself. Like I'll tell her not to say anything because people won't believe her, or that both of us will get into big trouble. Or, I say I'm sorry and it will never happen again. I might tell her that I'll deny it and her parents won't believe her. Usually the girl is confused and ashamed, so she doesn't tell anyone. I know I need help, but what would people think? What would happen to my career? I'd be ruined."

A priest who desires adolescent boys comments, "You tell me why I do what I do. I wish I knew. I like being with young guys and they like being with me. I help them by giving them experiences and opportunities they would probably never have. Usually I get involved with the boy's family. It's common for me to dine with them and even go on vacation with them. In short, they trust me. And everything seems to go well until I find myself wanting to get more intimate. I try to push those feelings out of my mind, and sometimes I'll succeed and nothing sexual occurs. At other times the kid simply grows up, or maybe outgrows me and drifts away. But sometimes I get sexually involved. It's not that I'm some kind of sexual maniac, but…

"I'm usually sexually attracted to a kid who is well built, athletic, and sensitive. Often he is a sullen or troubled fellow. Anyhow, I'm not lurking in the shadows waiting to pounce on someone. When I get sexually involved, I've usually known the boy for some time. We've done many things together, like going to ball games or cultural events. I'm like a father to him. Come to think of it, he calls me father. Then something happens. It's as if a mood gets the best of me, and I can't stop myself. Sometimes I feel it coming, and at other times it sneaks up on me. The boy is usually surprised and confused, though not always. I try to tell him that I really care for him, and not to let this get in the way. I know it's wrong, but what can I do?"

Although little is known conclusively about the causes of pedophilia, there are some research data and insights that help our understanding and treatment. It is estimated that 65% of pedophiles were victims of sexual abuse. Although biological factors may be present such as high testosterone levels, this is not always the case. Although few people with high hormone levels are sex offenders, an individual's biochemistry should be tested. In fact, some treatment programs use Depo provera to reduce the sex drive by lowering the production of testosterone.

All treatment models demand that such sex addicts have no involvement with children and adolescents, particularly when the offender is the only adult present. A pedophile who works with or spends considerable time with minors is like an alcoholic who tends bar or is a wine taster. Pedophiles and ephebophiles must abstain from private contact with minors.

Indeed, abstinence is essential for recovery. Like most sex offenders and others having addictive behaviors, pedophiles and ephebophiles learn to accept and manage their addiction. Although we do not know if a sex offender can cure or expunge his condition, most can enter a program of recovery. How to help oneself and others is the subject for the next chapter.

Chapter Ten
Helping Self and Others

An initial step in helping oneself and others is to distinguish between therapeutic help and normative evaluation. Normatively, lustful sex should neither be condoned nor recommended because it violates health. Our responsibility is to preserve and promote healthy norms as well as model them in behavior via teaching, writing, and conversation.

On the other hand, a therapeutic approach suspends normative evaluation in order to explore the sense and nonsense of sexual desires and actions. When asked or when it is our responsibility, we can offer our standards; otherwise, we accept (neither condoning nor condemning) less than healthy sex and encourage the person to enter the process of self disclosure and growth. With compassion, we accept the lustful person in the pursuit of healthy living.

For many reasons, it is difficult to help oneself and others. One impediment is our deficient programs for coping with and integrating sexual desires. We have seen that many of us are left with two options: to repress or to satisfy and that such a choice actually offers little freedom. We may be told to "integrate" sexuality, but few helpful suggestions are given for doing it. We have emphasized that our culture and mass media give spiritually impoverished models of sexuality. Furthermore, sexuality is an intimate experience that is not easily shared.

It is also important to be in touch with our own sexuality; otherwise, we can hardly help others. For instance, well-intentioned authorities who lack a healthy sexuality themselves are unlikely to help and more likely to enable sex offenders. So, we start with ourselves; then we can try to help others.

Realize that sex gives immediate rewards that reinforce the behavior and increase the likelihood of its occurrence. To use the parlance of learning theory, the stimulus-response bond is strengthened through repeated behaviors. The individual who masturbates compulsively, for example, is caught in a discouraging circle: the more he masturbates, the more difficult it is to control. Good intentions and will power are not enough to achieve abstinence because, in a sense, our body has a will of its own. Suppression, anticipation, sublimation, and integration of sexual desires as well as humor and prayer are significant in reducing the strength of habit.

Consider a man's approach. "When I'm tempted to log onto cybersex, I try to get busy or get involved with others. And when this is not possible, I try to keep God in the picture. Sure, I pray, but that's not all I mean. This may sound silly, but I really mean it when I say that I try to keep God's spirit in the person I'm fantasizing about, and I try to see God in me. When I let God stay in the picture, my experience is different. And when I forget about God, I have less power to resist. Then I am inclined to see myself and others as sexual bodies without spirit. I lust, and afterward, I feel spiritless."

Charting recurrent patterns of sexual activity may also be helpful For instance, an individual may discover regular times and places when and where cybersex is likely to occur. Anticipation that he is more vulnerable at certain times, in certain places, and in certain moods can help him to monitor and take better care of himself. He can take measures to safeguard his vulnerable self.

This man is aware of his vulnerability, and he anticipates and manages accordingly. "Since I know I'm especially vulnerable at night and on weekends, I'm especially careful at those time to be busy or to avoid getting preoccupied with the possibility of phone sex. It seems that when I am bored, lonely, or generally uptight, I am more prone to call. Not that it is terribly bad, but it is nothing to be proud of either. Besides, it is costly and a waste of time.

Kinds of guilt can be differentiated and discussed. Ideally, we can experience more than "superego" guilt, the kind that comes from breaking a rule, and in the extremes engendering feelings of damnation. We may tempted to act as children who follow the letter of the law or as adolescents who judge reality in terms of absolute ideals—either good or bad, meaningful or meaningless. Nevertheless, such cognitive (superego) guilt can remind us to abstain from inappropriate sexual behavior. Ideally, a more mature guilt comes from our spirituality.

Rather that feeling guilty primarily because of breaking a rule, guilt can stem from a violation of our spirit or a failure to become what we can become. Spiritual guilt calls us to appreciate the good and to seek a better life, not to focus primarily on the negative or what we did wrong. Formal, cognitive guilt is in service of and should develop into transformal, spiritual guilt. It is more mature to follow the spirit rather than the letter of the law. Spiritual guilt helps us to learn from our misdeeds in order to make healthy amends. Healthy guilt also combats narcissism and exploitation, while motivating us to foster a community of love.

Differentiating between healthy and toxic shame can also be relevant. In contrast to guilt that centers on "doing" something wrong, shame centers on the feeling of "being" wrong. Consider shame as the experience of being seen as painfully diminished We can be ashamed when we violate ourselves or others and thereby diminish our worth. Such healthy shame motivates us to do our imperfect best. Toxic shame diminishes and impedes being ourselves. In unhealthy shame, we get stuck in feeling worthless and unlovable, and we want to disappear rather than being motivated to become better. Toxic shame lessens our well being and even increases the likelihood of repeated lustful behavior. Why abstain when we are worth so little?

Good books on sexuality can be helpful. But, what is a good book? Knowing the so-called facts and possibilities, both pro and con, can help. Many books on sexuality, however, have questionable values. For example, authors who recommend masturbation as a healthy practice are proclaiming a value system—one that does not take a wholistic approach. Remember, most therapeutic approaches to sexuality exclude the spiritual dimension.

Books can often be better than movies. Films pressure us to move at their pace, and are often ageist and sexist. Books are likely to give us more leeway to assimilate at our pace. Furthermore, graphics can play havoc on unconscious desires and fantasies. When we watch pornographic films, we can give ourselves and others a false impression of openness. Intellectually we seem fine, but our unconscious and affective lives may present a different story. After the aura of openness is over, images and desires emerge in dreams, fantasies, and interpersonal relations that may hinder rather that help our sexual lives.

From our wholistic perspective, lustful sex is a challenge to growth. The challenge is to listen to and learn from uncomfortable feelings that underlie and motivate lust. Feelings of disembodiment, fatigue, loneliness, boredom, and depression say something about our lives. A sexual response to such feelings is inadequate. At best, it gives short-term relief, but eventually exacerbates discomfort. It is better to strive to see the spirit hidden behind and in lustful sex, to hear the spiritual call in sex to promote virtue in self and others.

A prerequisite is the intent to abstain from sex as well as to abstain from people, places, and things that evoke lust. For example, it is imperative for pedophiles and ephebophiles to abstain from any experiences with minors. For one who is addicted to pornography, it is mandatory to abstain not only from pornography but also from places where such materials are sold.

More difficult and important is to abstain from fostering lustful desires and fantasies. As we have stated, desiring another exclusively in terms of sex is an unrealistic and therefore inappropriate response to another. Sex offenders must constantly intend to abstain from looking at themselves and others as sex objects as well as from unhealthy desires and fantasies. Such internal abstinence is necessary to be on recovery from sexual pathology.

To stop lustful thinking and fantasies is not easy. We are call to detach from obsessive thought and attach to healthier thoughts. In twelve-step parlance, we must get our mind off "stinkin'" thinking." Psychologically, we can use strategies like "thought-stopping," replacing negative with positive thinking, and defocusing from lustful thoughts and refocusing on healthier ones. Socially, we can connect and share with friends, a support group, or a sponsor. And spiritually, we must be careful to avoid displacing God with sex, but instead to keep God in our sexual perception.

Coping mechanisms, which we have previously discussed, can be useful. For instance, it is wise for and addict to anticipate *when* he is likely to be sexually aroused as well as *what* and *who* evoke his addiction. It is prudent to sublimate sexuality before it becomes urgent. Surrendering to a Higher Power is wise and effective. As we have seen, prayer is healing.

HELPING SEX ADDICTS

A twelve-step approach toward recovery, like Sexaholics Anonymous, is strongly encouraged for anyone who is a sex addict. The twelve-step program is usually affective because it is structured, wholistic, and communal. The structured part of the program—the steps to recovery, the tradition for unity, and the concepts for service—pressure sex addicts to be honest and accountable.

Sex addicts, for instance, honestly admit they are powerless over their addiction and that their life has become unmanageable. They come to believe that God or a Higher Power can restore them to sanity, and they turn their lives and will over to the care of God. They implement these fundamental steps of recovery by sharing his faults with trusted people and God and by making healthy amends primarily by living an abstinent and healthy life and practicing these steps in all his affairs.

A twelve-step program is wholistic in that it deals with physical, psychosocial, and spiritual dynamics of recovery. Actually, few therapeutic approaches include the spiritual dimension, let alone making it the paramount dynamic. To surrender to a Higher Power that cares and guides the addict is unique. Finally, a twelve-step program is rooted in and supported by fellowship so that one is not alone in recovery. With these commitments and practices as a foundation, addicts regularly participate in group meetings where they share their experiences, strengths, weaknesses, and hopes, while they are accepted, understood, supported, and confronted. Members are also held accountable while receiving guidance and encouragement to persevere in the program.

Extended inpatient treatment that integrates a twelve-step approach is the ideal. Such intensive treatment is followed by a structured, life-long aftercare program that includes, at least initially, effective psychotherapy, a support group, spiritual direction, and an ongoing twelve-step program and meetings, follows such intensive treatment.

Recovery from sex addiction or any sexual problem goes beyond mere abstinence. Recovery means to become healthy not only with one's sexuality but also with life as a whole. Recovering persons not only abstain from compulsive sexual behavior that harms self and others but also learn to increase and value the worth of themselves and others. People in recovery learn to see, think, feel, judge, and live their life radically different. Sex offenders can be healthy and holy if they maintain and foster chastity as well as a program of recovery. Keep in mind that chastity literally means being pure, which includes abstaining from behaviors, thoughts, and fantasies that involve or lead to sexual offenses.

We must care for, treat, and give consequences to sex offenders as brothers and sisters. Their problems rarely come from willfulness; actually, they are more akin to alcoholics. Those who are caught in the quicksand of addiction ought to share their secret burden and seek help. Their way to freedom includes being medically sound, no involvement with minors or with their addictive activities, increased involvement with healthy peers, psychological insight, effective coping mechanisms, and living an active spiritual life. Such an approach can give many sex offenders the power to live chaste, healthy, and holy lives.

Let us not forget the victims. Most people care about and feel bad for victims of sexual abuse, but not many truly understand or appreciate their plight. The effects of sexual abuse rarely disappear completely. Although the effects can dissipate in time, scar tissue is left in place of wounds. To re-emphasize, since our sexual bodies include the spiritual, sexual abuses are more than physical. Sexual violation is an insult and a wound at the core of our being. Although our bodies heal, our spirits seek respect, retribution, and reconciliation.

Sex victims deserve and should get help to work through such feelings as rejection, shame, threatened sexual identity, impaired sexual development, guilt, anger, and confusion. Firm, clear, and compassionate advice can help affirm and orient the victim sexually. Unfortunately, the knee-jerk reactions of well-intentioned parents and other authorities are often harmful by exacerbating the pain, shame, and confusion of the sexual offense. For example, they may ask inappropriate questions, minimize or maximize the offense, fail to deal with the victim's feelings, blame the victim, avoid helping, enable the offender, or simply deny that anything happened. Usually, underlying harmful responses are shame, anxiety, fear, co-dependency, arrogance, ignorance, incompetence, or pathology.

It is imperative to affirm a person' dignity. Sincere love is needed to loosen the shackles of shame. But many victim's feel stained, often for life. They feel that something is radically wrong with their being. Still, most victims desire, demand, and deserve justice. To hear genuine sorrow from the perpetrator can be critical to one's dignity and healing, especially when the offender is a trusted acquaintance, cleric, teacher, relative, or parent. Unfortunately, such sorrow and amends are seldom given. Perpetrators and their enablers are reluctant to admit their pathology, let alone giving or working on genuine amends.

Keep in mind that abuse by clerics and other trusted authorities is very close to incest. And like families, religious leaders can deny, cover, or enable their sick brothers. Or they follow a moral model, absolving offenders of their sins, accepting a firm purpose of amendment, and giving a penance. To be sure, such a pastoral approach has truth, but it should not exclude sex offences as sick and criminal, deserving of help and punishment. An approach that integrates moral, psychological, and legal models is most effective.

Few if any post-traumatic stress disorders are worse than sex abuse. Victims of sex abuse, particularly of incest and rape, are usually victims for life. Most victims survive, but too many with too much cost. Some avoid true intimacy; some become counter phobic in attacking men (or women); and others try to undo their trauma by later engaging in the same behavior.

There are victims who courageously grow stronger through their suffering. Usually with individual and group help, they manage to heal—to recover their wholeness. Invariably, some form of spirituality is incorporated in their recovery. It seems that love from self and others severs their chains of shame. It is even possible for victims to reconcile with themselves and sometimes with the perpetrators. Recovering sex victims can become wounded healers who are models of hope, courage, and inspiration.

CHAPTER ELEVEN
SEXUALITY THROUGH THE LIFE CYCLE

To talk about healthy sexual behavior is relatively easy; to live it is another matter. In this chapter, a developmental approach shows how age-related factors can influence sexuality as well as how we can practice healthy sex.

Remember: Life is a dynamic process that is continually unfolding. Although we may try to stop change, we are always restive and restless—yearning for deeper meaning and fulfillment. At the moment of conception, we are thrown into the life cycle of birth and death. Life, including sex, is continually dying to a significant past and living toward a meaningful future to for a healthy present. Being an integral part of human existence, sexuality is a part of the life cycle of living and dying .

One approach to development is to chart stages throughout life. Although such an epigenetic approach is less precise in our later years, critical periods, moments of adjustment, and times of transition can still be normatively sketched. Even though these developmental stages may not fit any of us perfectly, they can serve as developmental guidelines.

In short, sexuality changes throughout life according to our situation, age cohort, inheritance, developmental stage, expectations, opportunities, health, etc. The present project is to discuss common developmental obstacles to and opportunities for healthy sexuality.

CHILDHOOD AND ADOLESCENCE

Despite considerable evidence, some people still have difficulty in admitting that sexuality exists in infancy and childhood. Indeed, the sexuality of childhood differs significantly from that of adolescents and adults. Being pre-genital and narcissistic, it tends to remain within the child in contrast to post-pubescent sexuality, which moreover seeks connection with another.

It is commonly accepted that the way parents and other significant people respond to children's sexuality impacts on later sexual development. A simple example is that punishing or shaming a child for playing with his or her genitals can set the infrastructure for later guilt and shame, or going to the opposite extreme, fostering genital play is likely to increase the likelihood of impulsive gratification. Indeed, extreme repression or expressions are precursors of trouble. A moderate approach, such as encouraging the child to be involved in another activity rather than punishing or rewarding genital play, is preferable. In short, the sexual responses and milieu in our early development significantly influence how we deal with our sexuality in later years.

Adolescence ushers in a plethora of subtle and blatant physical, psychosocial, and spiritual changes. Signs of sex are relatively rapid as manifested in height and weigh, hair, voice, genitals, seminal ejaculation, and menstruation as well as urgent sexual desires. Along with cognitive development from concrete operations to more formal and abstract intellectual functioning, adolescents look at and experience themselves and others differently.

Adolescence is a transitional time when one is no longer a child and not yet an adult. Understandably, adolescents can experience themselves as being in a quandary—too old to be children and too young to be adults, while feeling internal urges and external pressures to become sexual adults.

Spirituality also begins to emerge explicitly in contrast to its adumbrated presence in childhood. In early adolescence, spirituality initially and paradoxically usually surfaces in absence so that many young adolescents go through a period of negativity. They question almost everything, and nothing makes much sense. Typically they are bored and restless even though they have scarcely lived fifteen years. Still, their questioning of standards and values is part of developing their identity. Actually, their so-called negativity eventually leads to positivity, manifesting a common spiritual dynamic: absence leads to presence.

When new and intense sexual changes occur, adolescents may react with fear and curiosity, with pleasurable attention and embarrassment, or experience urges to share and withdraw. Many adolescents feel somewhere in the middle: moving both toward and away from sex. For most, sexuality becomes compelling and challenging. Without spiritual values, abstinence is practically meaningless or becomes mechanical rather than life-giving and liberating.

Unlike pre-puberty sex, sexuality now orients adolescents socially – to explore the possibility of sexual relations with others. A centrifugal force emerges in addition to the centripetal force of childhood sexuality. For some adolescents, genital experiences are more likely to occur in fantasy than in reality. Unfortunately, many adolescents engage in genital behavior long before their cognitive and spiritual functions can adequately cope. Since the attitudes and behaviors we develop in adolescence highly influence later development, adolescence is especially significant.

Early adolescent sexual development is difficult. Its newness and urgency as well as limited cognitive and spiritual abilities make it difficult to manage and integrate sexuality. Less than healthy social models and education compound the problem. Understandably, parents worry about their adolescent's sexuality. Although many adolescents get through this time without serious harm, many others short of healthy sexual development.

Abstinence can be particularly difficult to achieve for reasons like new and urgent desires, media and peer pressure, and cognitive and spiritual limitations. For instance, sometimes sexual urges can be so strong that adolescents seem to become mere sexual beings. Once caught in a sexual world, there seems to be no alternative but satisfaction or frustration. We have seen that to encourage repression or gratification is counter-productive, but to help them is not easy. In whatever case, often the value of abstinence is lost.

Keep in mind that young adolescents have not yet developed their identity and values, and some stop maturing because of drug addiction or other problems. To a large degree, young adolescents have to follow the values of adults until they personalize values within themselves. To compound matters, there are few persons and places where adolescents can go to question, explore, and develop healthy values. Most resources foster or forbid sexual behavior without giving healthy and relevant reasons for doing so.

One school of thought would contend that because of immature identity formation (such as a diffused, negative, or foreclosed identity), many adolescents lack the discipline, maturity, and value system that are necessary to abstain. Some people theorize that well-intentioned spoiling, though seemingly more humane than authoritarian restriction, promotes self-centeredness, low frustration tolerance, and lack of discipline. Others hypothesize that many adolescents fail to learn an awareness of and a responsibility for right and wrong behavior, or that they are exposed to a value system that fosters self-satisfaction, making it difficult to develop a healthy sex life. Consequently, when confronted with sexual urges, adolescents may have neither guiding principles nor the discipline to cope with the confusion of sexual self-discovery.

Many others contend that adolescents are more knowledgeable and freer than ever. Unlike in the past, they are offered sex education, mass media exposure, and opportunity for sexual experiences. Others would counter this view stating that adolescents are given too much too soon and that their freedom is actually license. Adolescents can too easily regress to a narcissistic posture of self-satisfaction, overtly rebel, escape from life demands, be too influenced by peers and mass media, or simply live a diffused and immature life.

Still, others point out that increasingly more young people are abstaining from genital behavior for health or religious reasons, or both. These adolescents and young adults choose to wait until marriage or until they are older to handle the consequences. Their abstinence does not seem to be born out of repression or other unhealthy defenses. Rather, they seem to be open to sex and choose not to seek gratification. In short, they abstain.

Moving to middle and late adolescence, sexuality remains an issue, particularly intimacy. We have seen that differentiating between sexuality (genitality) and intimacy (affection) can be very difficult, especially for males. For instance, it is often difficult for adolescent males to express or even feel tenderness and thoughtfulness, let alone promote these qualities as ends in themselves. If they do, they may be labeled as feminine and be rejected by many boys and girls as well. Interestingly, most girls/women value and want such affection without sex, but when they get it, some are skeptical, label it as gay or effeminate, or criticize and reject it.

During adolescence and emerging adulthood, boys learn to be men who value affection and intimacy as means to genital gratification. Most fail to learn the art of experiencing affection as end in itself and consequently intimacy is impeded. Girls who are becoming women, on the other hand, are more adept at experiencing affection as an end in itself as well as integrating sex and affection. To learn to experience and enjoy affection as an end in itself is one of the key ways to practice healthy sex and abstinence in adolescence as well as in later development.

Around sixteen or older, sexual identity and interpersonal relations become more crystallized and refined. By now, positive or negative ways to cope with sexuality have been learned, and there are more possibilities for sexual behavior. Although they can always be modified, one's attitudes toward and practice or rejection of sexuality are becoming more solidified.

Opportunities for sexual relationships, coupled with romantic idealism, can be seductive. For instance, some adolescents may want to give themselves wholly or "perfectly," including sexually. Or they can deceive themselves into thinking they have completely own their bodies and can do as they like. And although technology has made it easier to prevent pregnancy and childbirth, birth control is far from perfect. The number of adolescents who become pregnant is substantial. As we know, the only absolutely effective method to prevent pregnancy (and disease) is abstinence.

Since the views and values we form during adolescence, though modified and deepened, tend to carry us throughout life, the period leading to emergent adulthood is significant to future sexual development. Adolescents or persons of any age who are diffused or confused, have a negative identity, or for whatever reasons have not found themselves can easily be led by peer and cultural pressure to behave sexually. To say no to such pressure presupposes a strong identity and values. Young people who can "just say no" are actually saying yes to themselves. But people who lack a healthy identity will find it very difficult to say no in service of a yes—or, to abstain.

Many adolescents who have a religious orientation may find it easier to practice abstinence, especially if they receive support and guidance from both their parents and their religious community. Nevertheless, people need not necessarily be "religious" to develop solid virtues that enable them to choose abstinence. However, it is very difficult to develop a solid spirituality without learning a religion in childhood and adolescence. Parents who avoid exposing their children to religious instruction for whatever reasons are cheating and hurting their children's spiritual formation. Without spirituality, sexual abstinence is very difficult, meaningless, or less than healthy.

Adults have a responsibility to help adolescents form values that foster freedom and health. To achieve this goal, we must begin and end with ourselves. We cannot give what we do not have. To be healthy models and mentors, our thinking and behavior ought to be congruent. Stated differently, we must walk our talk. Otherwise, we give ambiguous and ambivalent messages, and consequently harm more than help.

Although living our values is important, we also have to learn to articulate them in ways that are understandable to adolescents. This is a difficult but crucial task. For example, to show and explain why and how abstinence can be a healthier way than gratification or repression is important. How many adults can do this? What religion effectively does this? In contrast, mass media does an effective job in convincing adolescents that sexual gratification is the way to go. Adults, in and out of religion, can counteract the media messages by giving relevant, concrete, and understandable reasons for abstinence. Without lecturing, badgering, or judging, we can share our experience, strength, and vision.

Adolescents who can practice healthy celibate sexuality are invariably freer and more mature than other adolescents. They not only avoid sexually transmitted diseases and pregnancy, but they also strengthen their freedom and identity. Taking and practicing a stand that is counter-cultural presupposes and reinforces personal and interpersonal strength. Furthermore, such a counter-cultural life can engender creativity—a different way of looking at and dealing with reality. Rather than conforming to ordinary standards, we are challenged to formulate and live according to an extraordinary vision.

EMERGING ADULTHOOD

Late adolescence blends into emerging adulthood—a time from the late teens through the twenties, when we are no longer adolescents but not quite full adults. Emergent adulthood is a time of exploration and experimentation—of changing life situations, expanding social roles, and developing personal and professional commitments. Most young adults make life commitments that carry them throughout life, not only career choices but also married, single, or religious life. Of course, to make commitments without a solid identity is precarious at best.

Soon after entering the threshold of adulthood, we often experience a personal passage. Our impetus for change is more internal than external, more personal than political. In the late teens or early twenties, many of us go through a rather intense period of self-evaluation when we are thrown back on ourselves and question our values, goals, past inheritance, people (especially parents and significant others), and life in general. Who am I? Whence do I come? Where am I going? All these and other classical questions become critically important, and initially, few satisfying answers emerge.

During this novitiate of adulthood, it is often the case that a period of darkness precedes the light of more established adulthood. A moratorium invariably comes before a committed life. Emerging adults often experience intense feelings of loneliness—a yearning to be understood by and to be with another. The intimate presence of another is experienced more in absence than in presence. It would be a mistake to judge such lonely emptiness as symptomatic of something wrong. Actually, such existential loneliness can be important and even necessary when it enables us to discover ourselves and eventually surrender ourselves in intimacy.

Similarly, we may feel alone—by ourselves, but not necessarily yearning for others. Such a mood can offer us the opportunity to listen to and reflect on life. And sometimes, we may feel alone and lonely—silently shouting without any response. Such loneliness and aloneness at any time of adulthood can be important in finding oneself, including one's sexual self. Questions about sexuality seek important answers.

Sexual questions abound. What and who is a woman? A man? How do men and women differ? How much and in what way do sexist role expectations influence me? What is the difference between sex and gender, and how do I integrate them? Who am I sexually? What kind of a man or a woman am I? How can I or should I express my affection? What is the meaning of sex in my life? What is love? Am I lovable? Can I love and be loved without sex? Is sexual gratification wise? Is abstinence a viable option?

Although we can confront similar issues as adolescents, we usually do not articulate them as clearly and strongly as we do in young adulthood. Part of adulthood includes being a mature sexual being. But what is mature sexuality? Not many healthy answers are given. The beginning years of adulthood are ones of self-discovery and self-surrender. Ideally, as emerging adults we come to face our sexuality in all its dimensions.

In our twenties, we enter the world at large to find our personal and professional vocation. Being "a legal adult" can open up opportunities on all levels including sexual ones. Freedom from parental and environmental restraints and freedom for whatever we choose at this time. The challenge to implement our sexual self becomes a daunting developmental task.

Sexuality in its genital form is a key area at this time. For most, sexual activity as well as non-marital pregnancies are peaking. Still, it is possible to postpone expression. We can be so busy studying, working, and finding ourselves that we forget about our sexual selves. Such postponement of sexual awareness though not the same as repression, is not usually a healthy way to work through and to integrate sexuality. Such people are to be confronted later with experiences that they should have faced earlier. Simply stated, if earlier stages of sexual development are repressed, postponed, or immaturely satisfied, later stages of sexual can be aversely affected.

Since there are more opportunities and expectations to engage in sexuality, to be celibate is not usually popular and seldom publicly sanctioned. Perhaps more for men than for women, celibacy is often something to hide rather than to proclaim. It takes health and courage to go against social expectations that encourage sexual behavior as part of being a normal adult.

Besides social expectations, the unsettling experiences of self-discovery can pressure young people to get sexually involved. For instance, sex may feel better than the loneliness, aloneness, and emptiness of self-discovery. Although sexual pleasure can be an accessible way to purge pain, it can also be a way of running from one's self in the guise of meeting self and other. Since uncomfortable experiences like loneliness are rarely supported as necessary for growth, we can be pressured to escape from or numb them. Unfortunately, we can impede our growth by pursuing questionable norms of health.

Likely changes of venue and lifestyle evoke new issues, including sexual ones. Consider those novices of adulthood who have rigidly controlled or repressed sexuality. If they move away from home, they will probably experience different people, values, pressures, and opportunities that challenge their sexuality. Their latent sexuality may suddenly burst forth when they enter new situations, easily evoking confusion, guilt, shame, and vulnerability. When the dam of sexual repression breaks and floods one's awareness, control is almost impossible.

In contrast, some adults who have had a history of indulgent and narcissistic behavior along with an immature identity may find themselves with a license to satisfy their sexuality. Some of these emerging adults feel entitled to get what they want. Some think that as long as they are "sincere and honest" they can engage in sexual relations. They fail to realize that sincerity and honestly do not guarantee healthy behavior. Others believe that "as long as I'm not hurting anyone," it's all right. They fail to define "hurt," and they assume that avoidance of hurt equals health. Furthermore, they tend to follow 17th century philosophical assumptions that refute 21st century philosophy and science. Though seemingly more open than their repressed peers, they also fragment and fail to integrate.

Nevertheless, healthy choice and control are possible and do occur. A few men and women enter religious life and accept celibacy as a way to implement their communal and spiritual life. Some young adults practice abstinence for relatively non-spiritual reasons like safety, simplicity, and efficiency. Others refrain from sexual gratification because of spiritual values like love, freedom, and commitment. Without denying the meaning of sexual involvement, all of them think that the better good is to abstain.

ESTABLISHED ADULTHOOD

Realizing that we are no longer young adults and becoming older in our thirties, life is experienced differently. Classic questions emerge again. Where have I been? What have I done? What is the best I can do? Have I grown older together in love with my spouse? Or, will I ever get married? The vowed celibate might ask: Is this the right life for me? Really, how spiritual am I? Do I know what it means to love and to be loved? Questions persist with few answers. Do I want to live the rest of my life the way I have been living? Is there more to life? Is this all there is?

Along with more awareness and freedom, women often function more assertively and autonomously. Unlike men who have reached their genital peak in their late teens or early twenties, women may become more genitally and affectively sexual so that sexuality increases and seeks deeper satisfaction and fulfillment. Women who try to integrate their sexuality with love, want more from sex.

Women are especially sensitive to intimacy. A woman may reflect on and wonder what has happened to her sexual life in the last ten years. She may question if her celibate dreams, honeymoon ideals, or marital goals have been fulfilled. In particular, celibates may feel that time is running short for sexual fulfillment while experiencing a new and greater surge of sexuality.

Women who are more in tune with the spirituality of sexuality can intimidate men who take sexuality simply as a means to genital pleasure. To demand more than the physical and to expect love to be concretely shown in daily living can indict and confuse an immature man. Women's assertiveness as well as their personal and social awareness can also intimidate men. Men may defend themselves by forcing women to be more submissive, or men may simply become submissive or avoid confrontation. Without knowing it, women may have surpassed men in sexual as well as overall development. In a culture that makes men the vanguards of sexuality, especially of genitality, men can be threatened by women who are more sexual than they are. Men can feel socially and personally impotent—less powerful than they though they were. Medication is an inadequate response to this existential powerlessness.

On the one hand, this time can be ripe for an affair. These adults are still young enough to get around and old enough to know how to get around, and if they are going to make a move, this is the time to make it. Single women may become aware of the many married men who we "willing" to enter a relationship with them. They may observe how easy it can be to enter a temporary relationship, while wondering if it is worth it. Men notice married women who are lonely, frustrated, and perhaps prime for an affair. Indeed, marital and celibate fidelity can be challenged.

Along with curiosity, loneliness can pressure a single woman into sexual relationships. The realization that she will never know and give to and receive from a man in sexual intimacy can evoke frustration and emptiness. When a woman feels that she has much to give and no one to give to, sometimes any man may seem better than no man. Generally, a man has a broader spectrum of choice in contrast to a woman who is left with men of a similar or older age. Although this sexist discrimination is decreasing, it is still difficult for a woman to marry a man who is considerably younger.

On the other hand, becoming older helps us to see through false myths. We begin to learn that sexuality is not all ecstasy or a panacea for life's problems. Dreams begin to vanish and are replaced with stark reality. Nevertheless, the frustration of a less than fulfilling life, the loneliness of absent love, and the feeling that time is starting to run out may motivate us to enter sexual relationships.

If sexual awareness and expression have been repressed or postponed, sexuality can explode in one's thirties. When such sexuality emerges, it is usually difficult to integrate and make meaningful. Although we may be or appear to be adult in most areas, we can behave like adolescents in our naïve and giddy approach to sexuality.

When moving in and out of repression or postponement, one can be easily seduced. For example, when a man who is sensitive to personal values, promises to love and cherish a woman as well as share his vulnerability, she may be more likely to giver herself sexually. Or he may use a "line" that it is all right if she abstains, for he "accepts" and "respects" her. Such a man plays on her guilt, betting that she will soon succumb to his "unselfish and sacrificial care."

Seasoned adulthood can also be a time to reaffirm, rekindle, modify, or nourish sexuality as well as a time to integrate sexuality and spirituality.

We can become more sensitive to the relationship of love and sexuality rather than maximizing its pleasurable and reproductive dimensions. As we grow older, we can see and respond to people as whole beings; we can experience the spiritual and aesthetic and not only the functional or physical dimensions of one another.

In this time of established adulthood, sexuality can mature. Celibates can become, more than ever, vital lovers. Instead of being a source of painful frustration, sexuality can promote spirituality. Married couples may also enjoy sex more than ever, especially if they have actively promoted their spiritual lives. For instance, a man can be careful to stay in good physical and spiritual shape so he can engage more freely in intimate relationships as ends in themselves as well as ones leading to genital sex. A woman can initiate genital sex, knowing that such sex can be a cause as well as a consequence of love. She can also help her husband learn to explore and enjoy the infinite possibilities of intimacy with and without genital sex. When we come to better sexual integration, we increase and experience better manhood or womanhood. We become mature sexual-spiritual adults.

MID-LIFE ADULTHOOD

Spring is a memory and summer is ending; autumn is approaching. Entering our forties is not exactly old, but for most of us it is nearing the halfway point in life. In mid-life, it is not uncommon to experience life in terms of its limits and to ponder the meaning of life Such a crisis of limits calls for ultimate responses, a leap into the unlimited. In short, the second half of life pressures us to deepen our spiritual life.

Besides experiencing our physical limits, the most radical limit: death—confronts all of us. Death demands to be heard, and its message is: Live! But how and why? Death summons us to take stock of our lives, or our reason for being. Part of this process is to make deeper sense of sex. To use sex to avoid coming closer to death only makes matters worse.

If we have not grown spiritually, our sexual experiences become boring and inadequate, or desperate. Consider mid-life couples who have become sexual strangers. The pressure for an affair is not rare. For instance, a man may deny being older by trying to look and act younger, to regress and be a Don Juan. Such regressive behavior is often an attempt to avoid intimate and ultimate questions.

Life's second half is an interior journey that includes facing and integrating the other sex within ourselves. In Jungian parlance, the *anima* in men and the *animus* in women demand to be heard. Besides avoiding the crisis of limits, many men have difficulties with becoming an androgynous person. Rather than regressing or avoiding this challenging issue, some men do integrate the female within themselves and become better men as well as achieving more understanding of and intimacy with women. In our framework, they grown in primary and affective sexuality.

Women can continue to intimidate men. Perhaps a woman's most significant power lies not in so much in what she does as in who she is. Women often do better with issues of androgyny. They are more likely to promote spiritual qualities like open and vulnerable sharing and loving, as well as being assertive and autonomous. When women minimize their spiritual power and compromise themselves, they, like many men, are really not powerful or free.

It may be difficult to cope with desires for intimacy. Loneliness and frustration can haunt them. Fleeting sexual experiences may give some temporary satisfaction but eventually leave them yearning for authentic and ongoing intimacy. Understandably, some desperately use sex as a way to escape the pain of a relatively loveless life. Instead of sex and love being integrated, sex can be a displacement of love. More importantly, sex calls for love, and loveless sex leads to elusive intimacy and continued disconnection. Indeed, it is better to abstain from sex that displaces love.

Mid-life is often a crucial time of assessing and readjustment to our life of love. We may strengthen and deepen our love, or we may take stock of past love and feel insecure about the future. Or we may simply adjust to each other's independence and go our separate ways. In whatever case, if we fail to promote a life of love, we fall out of love. Rather than having sex in a futile attempt to find love, we can take stalk of ourselves.

Resonate with this recently widowed woman who reflects on her sexual experience. "Well, it was three years ago when my husband died from a long and painful bout with cancer. Although his death was not sudden, it was difficult to watch him waste away. Jack's death was a relief for me, and I think for him, too. But, I felt his loss, and I still miss him, for we were very much in love.

"Jim has been a friend since my husband and I met him and his wife in college. And when Jim's wife succumbed to cancer six years ago, Jack and I gave him a lot of support. Little did I know that three years later I would be in a similar position. Now, it was Jim's turn to help me, and he did. Of course, he knew what I was going through better than anyone.

"Well, one thing led to another, and we got sexually involved. I never had intercourse with anyone except my husband. Not to make excuses, but, I think that common suffering unites people. There was a special and powerful bond between Jim and me. And, we were so lonely and hurting. Our romance eased our painful loss and gave new life. It felt good. So, why did I stop?

"It wasn't a matter that our relationship was bad, but I wondered where we were going. In the heat of passion, everything seemed fine and possible. I felt like a young adult again, like one of my teenage kids. When intimate, Jim and I were great. But outside of these precious times?...

"I thought of marriage, but Jack was still very much in my heart. I didn't want to be married simultaneously to two men. Furthermore, outside of intimacy, Jim and I had many differences, like our approach to child rearing, money, religion and God, parents, extended family, lifestyle, etc., etc. So, I decided that a moratorium was in order, and we separated.

"I miss Jim, but I think I made the right decision. I don't think marrying him would have worked. And I don't want sex without marriage. I get the feeling of being a mistress, albeit a good one. It's like having the icing without the cake. At first, it tastes delicious, but over time it's not substantial. Some people might say it's a lot better than nothing. I disagree. I got to have a cake with my icing."

Most people could empathize with this woman and understand her sexual involvement. When life is terribly unfair, sexual intimacy is comforting and life giving. The powerful forces of mutual suffering and powerlessness can bond people. Abstinence only seems to add to the unfairness and pain.

Yet, this woman chose abstinence, to use her metaphor, after enjoying the icing and probably some cake too. She paused and stepped back to see more broadly and deeply. She did not condemn her sexual involvement; she thought it was good. Having reflected on her everyday life and future, she concluded that she wanted a more substantial and consistent life. Grieving her loss, she decided to abstain from being physically involved— to give up something good for something better.

MIDDLE AGED ADULTHOOD

The fifties usher in another period of self-confrontation and re-evaluation. Even though we have been true to our values for a half-century, we may confront them again. The old but perennial questions reemerge: Who am I? Who am I going to be and what am I going to do with the remaining time? Have I made a real difference? How can I improve? Why am I here? Sexuality is not spared in this self-assessment What does it mean to be a middle aged man or woman? How does sex fit into my life? Do I love my spouse? Am I loved? What is intimacy and how do I find it as a single person?

We hope that this dark night will lead to light. However, while we are in darkness, we can feel anxiously empty and depressed. We probably experience a crucial truth—that we are closer to death than to birth. The voice of death continues to call for a life-inventory, which includes a sexual assessment.

Sexuality is a critical challenge. Again and again questions emerge: What is being a man? A woman? Have I been a true man/woman in my past life? Have I lived a healthy sexual life? Will I be a sexual being in the future? Have I missed sexual experiences that can no longer be experienced?

We can try to become "sexless" and become neuter. Some men continue their sexual atrophy, while not learning how to be simply affectionate. They have not learned the art of being abstinent in service of intimacy. Increasingly more middle-aged women are realizing that they need not become sexually invisible. Menopause need not be a sexual disaster wherein women accept the violent and false diagnosis of "change of life"—from being sexual to being neuter. More women are realizing that menopause can usher in a new sexual freedom. Yet, if sexuality is not attended to and integrated at this time, it can slowly disintegrate and atrophy. Then, abstinence is not a matter of choice, but is a symptom of an unhealthy condition.

If we have tried to exclude the spiritual side of our sexual selves, our fragmented style usually catches up with us at this time. We feel that something is terribly missing. If we have seen sexuality merely as a quantitative challenge rather than a qualitative relationship, sexuality dissipates. The monotony and poverty of physical sex becomes a boring routine. Or we may simply avoid sex by becoming preoccupied with our careers and economic pursuits.

As we get older, we feel a greater need to integrate sex and love—to experience spirit in sex. More than ever, sexuality calls for spirituality, and spirituality for sexuality. When we respond to this call, both sexual gratification and abstinence become better. Sexual relations become more intimate, richer, and lasting, and sexual abstinence becomes easier and more meaningful.

Contrary to cultural beliefs, it is possible to become more sexual as we grow older. Genital sex may not be as frequent as it was in the past, but its qualitative side can improve. If sexuality has been inactive or not integrated, then the prognosis for a healthy sexual life in the middle and elder years is poor, and abstinence becomes a negative coping mechanism. If sexuality has been creatively integrated, then the prognosis is favorable. We can grow more deeply in being androgynous men and women who can express intimacy with or without genital behavior.

Even the way we look and appear can be a call for spirit. Physical aging can be a call for and a challenge to show new spirit, depth, and vigor. Intimacy in terms of grace, gentleness, and tenderness can be a new form of vitality—in a sense: sexuality permeated with spirituality. Thus, the hand that is becoming wrinkled and spotted can have more spirit and beauty than the one that is twenty years old.

As we have indicated, the voice of death speaks clearly and loudly as we grow older. Death is a demand to live more fully, to go beyond life's periphery to the center of living. Thus even though some older people still try to run from authentic living, it becomes increasingly difficult, for death calls forth the spirit of sex in all of its dimensions.

ELDER YEARS

Some people assume that the elderly are all alike. Actually, the contrary is true: The older we get, the more unique we become. Some elders are very much alive and active, while others go more slowly but are just as alive. Others stay in neutral, avoid, and die earlier than their time. A broad continuum with considerable variation exists biologically, psychologically, socially, and spiritually. And, old people vary considerably in their sexuality.

To speak of sexuality in the elder years may sound contradictory and even repulsive. To imagine wrinkled bodies being sexually intimate evokes discomfort in some people. Nevertheless, sexuality is an important experience in old age. Actually, seniors can be the most sexual of all people insofar as they are becoming more authentic men and women. Furthermore, healthy elders can be more intimate with life, with self, with others, and with God. Although the urgency of genital sexuality decreases, sex still can be integrated and celebrated. In marriage, sexuality can be better than ever, and in single life, abstinence can become relatively easier and liberating.

Indeed, genital frequency and intensity usually decrease with old age. Although age is not a disease, illness that impedes sexual relations is more prevalent in old age. Along with overall health and biochemical changes, body-concept is significant. For instance, some old people become preoccupied with their physical limitations and fail to accept and give deeper meaning to their bodies in terms of affection and expression. Furthermore, elderly persons are likely to be single.

If we have not had sexual relations in the past, sexuality may not be a difficult issue. For example, vowed celibates who have led a healthy celibate and chaste life may be at peace with their abstinence. However, if vowed or involuntary celibates have repressed sexuality, loneliness may emerge and frustration may be both relieved and increased with masturbation. Or people who have repressed sexuality can end up being dried up, experiencing insipid emptiness and lethargy. Some old, single persons are open to and pursue sex, while others are sexually vibrant and abstinent celibates. Although physical capabilities are lessened, primary and affective sexuality as well as cognitive functions can be deepened more than ever.

In the elderly years, death embraces us and invites us to a better life. Can we come to a sense of reconciliation and integration—a serene wholeness? Specifically for our concern: Can we integrate and realize our sexuality? If we have lived the life of integrated (chaste) sexuality, then sexuality will fall into healthy place.

In the late phase of adulthood, although we may not "feel very old," we are usually treated as such. Despite ageism, we still feel young in our old bodies. If we have grown through the current of life, we will reach the climax of our lives. As "old elderly" people, we can come to the zenith of our primary and affective sexuality. We can refuse to follow false ageist scripts like "old people are neuter and lifeless." We can proclaim the deepest and paramount message of sexuality—that we are conceived to be with and for one another.

Genital sexuality, whether acted upon or not, calls forth and promotes the spiritual. Sublimation and integration can give us vitality and enthusiasm. Being unlikely to focus on physical sexuality, we can purposely and spontaneously "see" and appreciate the embodied beauty of ourselves an others. In this way, the spirituality of sexuality can reach its culmination in the elderly years.

For instance, consider older men who become more receptive and nurturing as well as more gentle and open to affectionate promptings. In a similar way, older women can become more receptive and open to assertive and individual drives while continuing to nurture their affective and expressive ways of coping with reality. Androgynous men and women can in many ways be more sexual than younger people.

Sexuality can help us become vitally beautiful persons in our last years. Even though our bodies may be disintegrating, we can show a new grace and sensitivity. When we witness to the deeper values of sexuality, we may threaten people who identify sexuality with pleasure. Elderly people can indict such shallow views and proclaim sex's deeper dimensions.

It is interesting to note that the sexes are more alike and more in harmony in the first and last years of life. It seems that some old people return to their origins. This is not to say they are the same as children or that they regress, but that they participate more wholly and fully in humankind. They transcend sexual dichotomies, prejudices, and other factors that prevent sexual integrity.

Yet, old people may threaten those who are not old because they are so close to death. Paradoxically, coming to the end can intimidate people, for death demands authentic living. Death questions life, including its most vital form—sex. Our being toward death proclaims that sexuality is more basic and goes far beyond mere physical pleasure and functional reproduction. It is the elderly who can call us to the spirit and beauty of sexuality.

The call of the elderly can be unsettling. Our reaction is to silence them, to neuterize them, to control them, to hide and forget them. To view and respond to the elderly as less than they really are, is to violate them, and therefore ourselves. When "we" make the elderly "them" instead of "us," we ought to feel painfully diminished.

However, when we dance with the elderly, we celebrate our sexuality and spirituality. Together we can listen to and move with the music of the Lord of the Dance. Ultimately, the climax of sex is the epiphany of the Spirit.

EPILOGUE

The recurrent theme of this book has been that integrative sexuality simply works better. To settle for being less than whole can indeed evoke short-term gains, but at the price of greater long-term losses. Although fragmented sexuality is commonly advocated and practiced today, it does not promote progressive health and lasting virtue.

Special emphasis was placed on the spirituality of sexuality and on the sexuality of spirituality. To try to engage in sex without spirit is humanly understandable but not recommended, for the consequences of spiritless sex are fragmentation, emptiness, and alienation. Spirituality without sexuality is insipid, constricted, and distant. In either case, being less than whole wastes precious time and energy and fails to give integral growth of sex-and-spirit.

In short, we are both sexual and spiritual creatures; one without the other makes us less than God intends us to be. God calls us to use our minds and wills to maintain and nourish our sexual selves in congruence with authentic spiritual values. How we do this will depend on our vocational life-style—married, single, or vowed celibate—as well as individual and environmental factors. Whatever our situation, we are foolish to pursue less than wholistic sexual lives.

The saving grace in this adventure is that we are in it together. We are not isolated individuals alone in our efforts; rather, we are integral members of the same community of humankind. The more you and I grow in healthy sexuality, the more we will positively impact and help each other.

It is eminently wise to acknowledge a Power that is greater than and yet intimately related to us—a God who will help us on our journey. To deny God, however we understand God, is to reject a Power that is the source of and means to healthy and holy sexual/spiritual living. To turn over our minds and wills to the care of God is a wise and practical decision. This choice gives us the vision and strength to become whole and holy mavericks who celebrate and live the unity of sex-and-spirit.

TERMS FREQUENTLY USED

Abstinence. Behavior that refrains from gratifying genital desires.

Affective sexuality. Feelings, moods, and emotions that lead to and/or involve intimacy.

Androgynous. Manifesting characteristics of both men and women.

Anima. An inner feminine part of the male personality.

Animus. An inner masculine part of the female personality.

Badness. Behavior that intends to violate love and/or community growth and welfare.

Bisexuality. Erotic desires for and/or genital gratification with both men and women.

Chastity. The practice of sexuality with healthy motives and actions.

Community. Being in union with or being an integral part of the same system: I-you-God are essentially interrelated.

Embodiment. Being incarnated; physical.

Femininity. The way a woman has learned to manifest herself and the cultural roles of being a woman.

Genital behavior. Actualizing one's genital desires with self or another.

Genitality. Genital feelings, thoughts, desires.

Genital sexuality. Behavior, thoughts, fantasies, desires, and feelings that activate the genital organs.

Gender. The condition of being primarily female or male.

Goodness. Behavior that is congruent with and fosters healthy love.

Healthy. Behavior that is congruent with and fosters wholistic growth.

Heterosexual. A person who finds himself or herself oriented towards erotic preference for the other sex.

Heterosexuality. Sexual relationship—primary, affective, or genital—between a man and a woman.

Homosexual. A person who finds himself or herself oriented toward erotic preferences for the same sex.

Homosexuality. Behavior that leads to or involves genital gratification with the same sex;

Homosocial. Primary and/or affective sexual involvement with the same sex.

Integration. To make whole. To perceive and appreciate the unity of body, mind, and spirit.

Intimacy. Self-disclosure and sharing. Personal and interpersonal closeness.

Love. To choose (rationally and/or transrationally) to foster the well being of community.

Madness. Being closed to experiences that are significant to and necessary for wholistic/healthy growth.

Masculinity. The way a man has learned to manifest himself and/or the cultural roles of being a man.

Negative defense mechanism. Processes by which we protect ourselves against unpleasant or anxious feelings that threaten to expose an unacceptable part of ourselves; e.g., repression, denial, rationalization, etc.

Nonhealthy. A lack of healthiness or wholeness.

Normality. Maintaining oneself and coping effectively with the everyday demands of reality.

Normal madness. Functioning within the confines of normal society without pathological symptoms, but still being closed to realities (e.g. spiritual ones) necessary for healthy living.

Pedophilia. A sexual disorder in which a minor is the love object.

Physical dimension. The structure and dynamics of a person's embodied-incarnated self. The pre-rational lived body.

Pornography. Anything, particularly mass media, whose primary purpose is to excite us genitally.

Primary sexuality. How men and women experience reality because of nature and nurture.

Psychosocial dimension. The structure and dynamics of functional ego activities that center around task-oriented behavior, coping, and cognitive processes. The rational self.

Sex. The inherited conditions that predispose and codetermine how as men and women we relate to reality.

Sexuality. How we relate to objects, events, and persons by virtue of being primarily men or Women.

Spiritual dimension. The structure and dynamics of experiences rooted in mystery, paradox, transcendence, and communal harmony. The transrational self.

Spirituality. The art of maintaining and promoting good and transrational experiences.

Wholistic. The ongoing integration of the physical, psychosocial, and spiritual dimensions of human experience.

BIBLIOGRAPHY

Angier, Natoli. *Woman.* N.Y.: Houghton Mifflin, 1999.

Beatty, Melody. *Co-dependent No More.* Center City, MN: Hazelden Publishing, 1987.

Beisky, Janet. *The Adult Experience.* St. Paul, MN: West Publishing Co., 1997.

Bradshaw, John. *Healing Your Shameful Self.* Deerfield Beach, Fl.: Health Communications, Inc., 1988.

Buber, Martin. *I and Thou.* New York: Charles Scribner's Sons, 1958.

Buytendijk, Frederik J. *Woman: A Contemporary View.* Translated by Denis J. Burrett. New York: Newman Press, 1968.

Chopra, Deepak. *The Spiritual Laws of Spiritual Success.* San Rafael, CA: New World Library, 1994.

Clark, Keith. *Being Sexual...And Celibate.* Notre Dame, IN: Ave Maria Press, 1986.

Cobb, Nancy J. *Adolescence: Continuity, Change, and Diversity.* Fourth Edition. Mountain View, California: Mayfield Publishing Co., 2000.

Cozzens, Donald B. *The Changing Face of the Priesthood.* Collegeville, MN: The Liturgical Press, 2000.

Cummings, Charles. *Eco-Spirituality Toward a Reverent Life.* New York: Paulist Press, 1991.

Daniluk, Judith C. *Women's Sexuality, Across The life span.* New York: The Guilford Press, 2003.

De Mello, Anthony. *Awareness.* New York: Doubleday and Co., 1990.

Diagnostic and Statistical Manual of Mental Disorders. Fourth Edition. Washington, D.C.: American Psychiatric Association, 1994.

Eagley, Alice H. and Wendy Wood. " The Origins of Sex Differences in Human Behavior." IN.: *American Psychologist.* June. Vol. 4, No.6, pp. 408-423

Eckhart, Meister. *Everything as Divine. The Wisdom of Meister Eckhart.* Translated by Edmund Colledge and Bernard McGinn. New York: Paulist Press, 1996.

Edwards, Denis. *Jesus and the Cosmos.* New York: Paulist Press, 1991.

Erikson, Erik H. *Identity: Youth and Crisis.* New York: W.W. Norton and Co., 1968.

Farrer-Halls, Gill. *Buddhist Wisdom.* Wheaton, IL: Quest Books, 2000.

Ferguson, Kitty. *The Fire in the Equations: Science, Religion, and the Search for God.* Grand Rapids, MI: William B. Eerdmans Publishing Co., 1994.

Foley, et.al. *Sex Matters for Women.* N.Y.: The Guildford Press, 2002.

Fox, Matthew. *Sins of the Spirit, Blessings of the Flesh.* New York: Random House, 1999.

Francoeur, Robert T. *Becoming a Sexual Person.* New York: Macmillan Publishing Co., 1991.

Fromm, Erich. *The Art of Loving.* New York: Harper and Row Publishers, Inc., 1974.

Gillian, Carol. *In a Different Voice*. Cambridge: Harvard University Press, 1982.

Goergen, Donald. *The Sexual Celibate*. New York: Harper and Row Publishers, Inc., 1975.

Greer, Germaine. *The Female Eunuch*. New York: Bantam Books, 1972.

Groeschel, Benedict. *The Courage to be Chaste*. Mahwah, NJ: The Paulist Press, 1985.

Hannnarskjold, Dag. *Markings*. Translated by Leif Sjoberg and W.H. Auden. New York: Alfred A. Knopf, Inc., 1964.

Heidegger, Martin. *Being and Time*. Translated by John Macquarrie and Edward Robinson. New York: Harper and Row Publishers, Inc., 1962.

Hillman, James. *The Soul is Code*. New York: Random House, 1996.

Hyde, Janet and J. DeLamato. *Understanding Human Sexuality*. Boston: McGraw Hill, 1997.

Johnson, Robert A. *SHE: Understanding Feminine Psychology*. New York: Harper and Row Publishers, Inc., 1986.

Johnson, William. *Mystical Theology. The Source of Love*. New York: Harper Collins Publishers, 2002.

Johnston, William. *Silent Music: The Silence of Meditation*. New York: Harper and Row Publishers, Inc., 1979.

Kasl, David, Charlotte. *Women, Sex, and Addiction*. N.Y.: Harper and Row, 1989.

Kraft, William F. *A Psychology of Nothingness*. Philadelphia: The Westminster Press, 1973.

Kraft, William F. *The Normal Alcoholic*. New York: Alba House, 1999.

Kraft, William F. *The Search for the Holy*. Pittsburgh: Cathedral Publishing, 1999.

Kraft, William F. *When Someone You Love Drinks Too Much*. Ann Arbor: Servant Publications, 2002.

Kraft, William F. *Whole and Holy Sexuality*. St. Meinard, IN: Abby Press, 1989.

Kraft, William F. *Ways of the Desert. Becoming Holy Through Difficult Times*. New York: The Haworth Pastoral Press, 2000.

Kurtz, Ernest and Katherine Kefalam. *The Spirituality of Imperfection*. New York: Bantam Books, 1992.

Laing, R.D. *The Politics of Experience*. New York: Pantheon Books, Inc., 1957.

Lightman, Alan. *Ancient Light: Our Changing View of the Universe*. Cambridge: Harvard University Press, 1996.

Lindberg, Anne Morrow. *Gift From the Sea*. N.Y.: Pantheon, 1995.

Luijpen, William A. *Existential Phenomenology*. Pittsburgh: Duquesne University Press, 1969.

Mackay, Judith. *The Penguin Atlas of Human Sexual Behavior*. New York: Penguin Putnam, Inc., 2000.

Maloney, George. *On the Road to Perfection: Christian Humility in Modern Society*. Hyde Park, New York: New City Press, *1995*.

Maslow, Abraham H. *Toward a Psychology of Being*. Princeton, NJ: D. Van Nostrand Co., 1968.

Masters, William H., Virginia A. Johnson, and Robert C. Kolodny. *Biological Foundations Of Human Sexuality*. New York: Harper Collins College Publishers, 1993.

Masters, William H. and Johnson, Virginia E. *The Pleasure Bond: A New Look at Sexuality and Commitment*. Boston: Little, Brown and Co., Inc., 1975.

May, Gerald G. *Addiction and Grace*. San Francisco: Harper and Row, 1989.

May, Rollo. *Love and Will.* New York: W.W. Norton and Co., 1969.

McCarthy, Barry and Emily. Rekindling Desire. *A step-by-step Program to Help Low-Sex and No-Sex Marriage.* N.Y.: Braumer-Routledge, 2003.

McNamara, William. *Mystical Passion: Spirituality for a Bored Society.* Mahwah, NJ: Paulist Press, 1977.

Moore, Thomas. *Care of the Soul.* New York: Harper Collins, 1994.

Moore, Thomas. *Soul Mates.* New York: Harper Collins, 1994.

Moore, Thomas. *The Soul's Religion. Cultivating a Profoundly Spiritual Way of Life.* New York: Harper Collins, 2002.

Norwood, Robin. *Women Who Love Too Much.* New York: Jeremy P. Tarcher, Inc., 1985.

O'Murchu, Diarmuid. *Quantam Theology: Spiritual Implications of the New Physics.* New York: Crossroad, 1997.

O'Murchu, Diarmuid. *Religion in Exile A Spiritual Homecoming.* New York: The Crossroad Publishing Co., 2000.

Oraison, Marc. *The Human Mystery of Sexuality.* Kansas City, MO: Sheed and Ward, 1967.

Paul, Margaret. *Do I Have to Give Up Me to Be Loved by God.* Deerfield Beach: Health Communications, Inc., 1999.

Paul, Margaret. *Inner Bonding.* San Francisco: Harper and Row, 1990.

Polkinghorne, John. *One World. The Interaction of Science and Theology.* Princeton: Princeton University Press, 1986.

Royda, Crose. Why *Women Live Longer Than Men.* San Francisco: Jossey-Bass Publications, 1997.

Runting, Susan J. *Human Sexuality.* (24th Edition). Guiford, CT: Dushkin/ McGraw-Hill, 1999.

Sex and Love Addicts Anonymous. Boston: The Augustine Fellowship-Wide Services, Inc., 2003.

Sexaholics Anonymous. Simi Valley, California: SA Literature, 1989.

Sheehy, Gail. *The Silent Passage.* New York: Pocket Books, 1991.

Silverstein, Louise B. and Carl F. Auerback. Deconstructing the Essential Father.: In. *American Psychologist.* June, Vol. 54, No.6, pp. 397-407, 1999.

Sobosan, Jeffrey G. *Romancing the Universe. Theology, Science, and Cosmology.* Grand Rapids, MI: Wm. B. Eerdmans Publishing Co., 1999.

Sullivan, Harry Stack. *The Interpersonal Theory of Psychiatry.* New York: W.W. Norton and Co., Inc., 1968.

Szuchman, Lenore T. and Frank Muscarella (Eds). *Psychological Perspective on Human Sexuality. New York:* John Wiley & Sons, Inc., 2000.

Tannen, Deborah. *Why Don't you Understand?* N.Y.: Morrow, 1990.

Tillich, Paul. *Love, Power, and Justice.* New York: Oxford University Press, Inc., 1954.

Travis, Carol. *Mismeasure of Woman.* New York: A Touchstone Book, 1992.

Van Kaam, Adrian. *"The Fantasy of Romantic Love,"* Modern Myth and Popular Fancies. Pittsburgh: Duquesne University Press, 1961.

Von Hildebrand, Dietrich. *Man and Woman.* Ann Arbor, MI: UMI Research, 1966.

Weideger, Paula. *Menstruation and Menopause.* New York: Dell Publishing Co., 1977.

Weinberg, George. *Society and the Healthy Homosexual.* New York: Doubleday, 1973.

Wilber, Ken. *The Marriage of Sense and Soul.* New York: Random House, 1998.

Woititz, Janet. *Healing Your Sexual Self.* Deerfield Beach, Fl.: Health Communications, Inc., 1989.